A Natural History

OF

LAKE
ONTARIO

A Natural History

OF

LAKE
ONTARIO

SUSAN P. GATELEY

THE
History
PRESS

Published by The History Press
Charleston, SC
www.historypress.com

Front cover, top: author collection; *all others*: photo by Susan P. Gateley.
Back cover: photos by Susan P. Gately.

First published 2021

Manufactured in the United States

ISBN 9781467147927

Library of Congress Control Number: 2021937065

Notice: The information in this book is true and complete to the best of our knowledge. It is offered without guarantee on the part of the author or The History Press. The author and The History Press disclaim all liability in connection with the use of this book.

In Memory of Roland Micklem
a teacher and naturalist
of compassion
insight
and humor

CONTENTS

ACKNOWLEDGEMENTS

Many people have assisted in creating the knowledge that made this book possible. In particular, I would like to thank Nick Eyles, Diane Dittmar and Gerry Smith for fact checks. And I also must express my gratitude to Betsy McTiernan, Iria and Juha Cantori, Pat Campbell and Marsha Sawma, my fellow beach walkers, whose sharp eyes saw much that I missed. I also must thank Chris Gateley and his entire family of Ogden descendants, who made it possible for me to explore our amazing lake and its shores over the years.

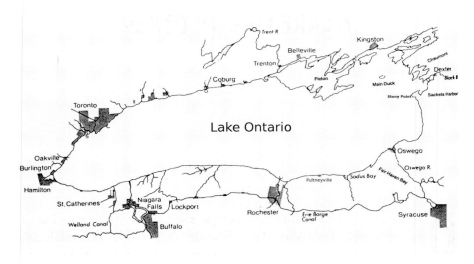

Map of Lake Ontario. *Figure supplied by Chris Gateley*.

A LAKE LIKE NO OTHER

Does it have a tide?" More than one person has asked this question on first viewing Lake Ontario. Its wide waters do seem almost oceanic, but they are not. Rather, freshwater lakes are among the most ephemeral of all geologic features. With a few exceptions, such as the Rift Lakes of Africa and Siberia's Lake Baikal, the lives of the world's lakes are no more than a brief blink on the planetary timeline. As soon as a lake is formed in Upstate New York, it begins to fill in to become a marsh, then a meadow and then a woodland. Nearly all of the world's lakes are located in the northern hemisphere, where Ice Age glaciers formed them, and they are no older than the time of the retreat of the last glacier.

Surface fresh water accounts for an exceedingly small percentage of the world's total water supply. Less than 1 percent of our water is contained in rivers and lakes, an amount roughly equivalent to a single drop in a bottle of wine. So the Great Lakes are truly a wonder and a gift to be treasured. They are the largest freshwater ecosystem on the planet and contain enough water to cover the entire United States to a ten-foot depth. Yet only about 1 percent of that volume is renewed each year. If more than that amount is removed or diverted for irrigation or some other purpose, lake levels will drop permanently.

Lake Ontario, the smallest by surface area, is unique among the "Five Sisters." It alone was once connected directly to the sea, and for a time, as the glacier retreated, marine animals were able to travel up the St. Lawrence River to reach its basin. Fossil remains of marine seals and fishes

Lake Ontario, the smallest of the five Great Lakes, still ranks in the top twenty of the world's freshwater bodies at number fourteen. *Author collection*.

and invertebrates from ten thousand years ago have been found in southern Quebec and eastern Ontario Province, marking the presence of a saltwater "Champlain Sea." During this time, several marine species, including the deepwater sculpin and the Atlantic salmon, made their way into Lake Ontario. Our lake is also unique among the Great Lakes in that much of its economic and cultural history is dominated by Canada rather than the United States. The French first settled Upper Canada (Ontario Province in 1673) well before British settlement on the south shore at Oswego, and today, more than 20 percent of Canada's population resides within a few miles of the lake's shoreline. In this corner of the continent, Canadians outnumber Americans by about ten to one.

Events on Lake Ontario, the Niagara River, and neighboring Lake Erie helped spark federal legislation to protect America's waters nationwide. The Clean Water Act; the Toxic Substances Control Act; and the Comprehensive Environmental Response, Compensation, and Liability Act (commonly known as the Superfund Act) were all crafted in large part after events in our region raised awareness of the dangers of various forms of pollution to human health. And that legislation and regulation also cleaned up some of the worst toxic messes in the Great Lakes watershed. Today, Lake Ontario faces a new set of challenges to its ecological well-being. But dozens of organizations and thousands of individuals are working to protect our inland sea. While plenty of threats to the lake's health remain, progress and healing have taken place, and this is still a place of incredible beauty filled with abundant life. And you can still watch those creatures, from tiny midges to soaring eagles and mighty sturgeon, as they continue to weave the web of life in and around one of the greatest lakes in the world. So slip on your walking shoes, cast off the dock lines to set sail or head for the nearest swim beach and enjoy a lake like no other.

1

THE AGE OF ICE

Lake Ontario lies in a land shaped by ice and water. Ours is a topography of kames, moraines, kettles, drumlins and prehistoric beaches. The vast ice sheet that covered this area ten thousand to twenty thousand years ago continues to impact us today. When the farmer discs and plants his field with the rocky knoll and the sandy patch of soil, or when the gardener or the hole digger struggles with cloddy sticky clay, they are reliving that glacial history. And those of us who rely on a shallow well for our drinking water may be benefiting from the last Ice Age's deposits that now form our aquifer.

The last major advance of ice here began about eighteen thousand years ago. At their maximum extent, glaciers completely covered all of present-day Lake Ontario and extended just south of Cayuga and Seneca Lakes. Studies suggest that when it finally melted, the ice retreated considerably faster than it had advanced. Nor was the retreat a simple one-way action. There were milder spells and colder times when the ice paused or even re-advanced some distance.

No one really knows for certain what caused that first unusually cold, snowy year when spring never came. Perhaps it was massive volcanic eruptions, like that of 1815, the year without a summer, when Tamboro erupted in the East Indies and blew two hundred cubic kilometers of earth into the air, sending enough ash into the atmosphere to block sufficient sunlight to tip the delicate global balance toward cooling. Or perhaps fluctuations of solar energy output or wobbles in earth's orbit triggered the Ice Ages. In any event, glaciers form from snow. And the heaviest snowfalls occur at temperatures not far below freezing, so it only took a slight drop in the overall average temperature on earth to initiate the last Ice Age. Geologists don't know for certain what triggered the last Ice Age—or its end. But we do know that profound shifts in climate can occur with staggering speed. Some studies suggest that the Ice Age ended with massive floods as the planet warmed over a period of as little as a decade or two.

Whatever the cause, the amount of ice that came grinding and scraping and slowly flowing across this landscape heading southwest from an origin somewhere around Labrador was almost inconceivable. The tremendous weight of up to two thousand feet of ice actually depressed the earth's crust hundreds of feet, causing it to tilt slightly toward the thicker ice to the north. Later, as the ice melted and retreated, the land bounced back to its original level. Because the ice was thicker and heavier to the north and slower to melt, it pushed the earth's crust down farther than it did on the lake's south shore. When the ice melted, the more depressed crust to the north rose more quickly. This tilted the entire lake basin slightly from north to south, lowering the land and raising the water along the south shore to flood valleys previously carved by south shore creeks and rivers during the great floods. These so-called drowned river valleys formed the half dozen present-day south shore bays between Rochester and Oswego. Parts of the St. Lawrence Valley rose several hundred feet, while the land on the south shore has rebounded over one hundred feet since the time of prehistoric Lake Iroquois.

A series of glaciers gouged out the Great Lakes and many other valleys and depressions, like those of the Finger Lakes just south of Lake Ontario. After the last ice sheet melted, it left a vast load of gravel and rock along the edge of its farthest advance. This ridge of gravel and rocks, known to geologists as a moraine, blocked the Finger Lakes and Ontario from draining south into the Mississippi River.

At first, Lake Ontario drained southwest of Syracuse. Later, it drained eastward through the Mohawk Valley as the St. Lawrence outlet was still blocked by ice. At that time, the lake's level lay over one hundred feet above its modern-day level, and its shoreline was several miles south of the present-day shoreline. That prehistoric shoreline's traces are still visible along old Ridge Road, a beach berm thrown up by the waves of Lake Iroquois. That berm extends from Sodus Bay to the Niagara River. This natural feature became a game trail used by animals and early indigenous inhabitants. Later settlers widened and improved the road, and it became a vital military and transport corridor. By 1820, just before the Erie Canal's construction, it was

Little Sodus Bay, one of a half-dozen drowned river valleys found on the lake's south shore. *Photo by Chris Houston.*

the main route westward from the Genesee River. It lives on today marked by a string of towns and villages between Lewiston and Wolcott.

When the last glacier retreated across New York, a very different flora and fauna from that of today followed it. At first, the climate was much like today's Canadian tundra. Bones of musk ox, arctic fox and caribou, as well as those of other creatures like the mastodon, have been found in Upstate New York peat bogs. People lived here, too, and may have played a major role in the disappearance of some of the now-vanished Pleistocene creatures that walked on the shore of Lake Iroquois. An intriguing note in one of Pierre Charlevoix's eighteenth-century accounts hints at their presence. He writes of an ancient Indian legend from a St. Lawrence–area tribe about a mythical creature long since vanished from the land. The Indians called it a great elk. Charlevoix wrote: "His legs they are so long that eight feet of snow are not the least encumbrance to him. His hide is proof against all manner of weapons, and he has a sort of arm proceeding from his shoulders which he uses as we do ours." Sure sounds like an Ice Age mastodon to me.

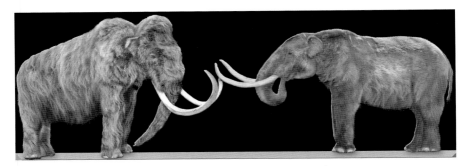

Mammoth (*left*), Mastodon (*right*). A number of mastodon remains have been exhumed from areas just south of Lake Ontario. *Wikipedia.*

The so-called Paleo people had reached Lake Ontario's shores within a few centuries after the ice's retreat. Some of their early campsites have since been submerged by changes in lake levels, but a few sites have been found and studied, including several from around present-day Oneida Lake that were probably once close to the south shore of Lake Iroquois. Fossil pollen records show a land of spruce and sedge giving way to pine and birch and then to a predominantly deciduous forest throughout the region as the glacier retreated. The vegetation changes reflect major climate shifts that these pioneering inhabitants had to contend with, including the cool-down period known as the Younger Dryas. But they persisted, switching from mastodon, bear-sized beaver and caribou roasts to moose and deer dinners as the landscape changed. Some archaeologists suggest that they were efficient enough hunters to eliminate the mastodon, giant ground sloth and the giant beaver from the land. These Paleo people also almost certainly relied to a considerable extent on fish, as did the Haudenosaunee clans who arrived much later, probably from the southwest. Of course, Paleo folk would also have foraged for nuts, berries, tubers and other edible plants, as did the tribes that came after them.

When the melting ice freed the St. Lawrence River channel, the Great Lakes drainage abruptly shifted to today's pattern, and the lake levels quickly dropped to approximately present-day levels. The land was still depressed from the glacier's weight, however, and so lay considerably below its present elevation. In fact, the St. Lawrence River and Lake Ontario were actually briefly below sea level for a time, and it was then that the lake experienced its so-called marine invasion. Salt water along with a number of marine creatures then entered the present lake basin. As the land rebounded from the ice's weight, the lake basin rose above the sea, and the lake once again became a freshwater sea. However, some of the marine fish, like the Atlantic salmon and the planktonic shrimp-like *Mysis*, managed to adapt to fresh water and so remain in the lake today. Additional evidence of the marine invasion comes from seal and whale bones found in sand and gravel deposits in the St. Lawrence Valley.

The glacier's movements made the south shore cobble beaches more varied than those on the Canadian shore. When I explored the northeastern coast of the lake during my first cruise to Canada in 1980, I was immediately struck by the monotony of its beach pebbles; they were nearly all gray. The south shore beaches I had grown up near were a colorful mix of brown, gray, black, white, orange and pink pebbles.

We owe that variety to the vast piles of glacial till, an unsorted mixture dragged along and dropped by ice. Till is made of sand, clay, rocks and boulders. It originated from various locations in the St. Lawrence Valley, the Adirondacks and Canada and moved south with the ice.

However, the land up near Chaumont and Henderson Harbor and that of some Canadian beaches and islands on the northeast side of the lake was stripped of most of its till during the last Ice Age. Here, the glacier scraped the land down to limestone bedrock. Scientists disagree on the reason why

South-shore pebbles are a diverse mix of rock types, as seen here on a beach near Port Bay. *Author collection.*

there is so little soil here. The bedrock may have been swept clean by fast-moving ice or perhaps by a cataclysmic drainage of glacial meltwaters. One website suggests that perhaps the soil and meltwater were swallowed up by abundant fissures and cracks in the limestone. Whatever the process, today, the pebble beaches here are mostly made up of bits and pieces of underlying bedrock and are uniformly gray.

A few miles inland from the Chaumont area are regions known as alvar barrens, where limestone bedrock and thin soils support unusual plant communities. Walking the old road to the lighthouse on the Canadian Park Island of Main Duck with its utterly flat expanse of bedrock, it's easy to see where the term *pavement barrens* came from. The Nature Conservancy maintains a preserve outside of Chaumont mainly because of the rare plants that survive in this prairie-like grassland mixed with scrubby white cedar and other trees. A striking feature of the "pavement" areas are the straight-lined cracks, joints and fissures that run through the flat bedrock. It's a harsh place to make a living as a plant, as the "pavement" alternates between being flooded by heavy rains and baked dry by summer sun. Yet, some unusual plants manage to grow here, among them a rare flower known as the prairie smoke, thought to be found nowhere else in New York State.

The glacier is also responsible for the presence of the drumlins that are so characteristic of the region between Syracuse and Rochester. Drumlins are distinctively sculpted hills of glacial till. They are all oriented roughly north–south following the flow of the glacier and have a streamlined, elongated appearance, with the north ends being steeper and the south ends tapering gradually down. From the air, they look a bit like streamlined nacelles or perhaps like a school of swimming fish.

Between Sodus and Oswego, a number of drumlins meet the lakeshore, and as that shoreline erodes into their ends, it creates a series of distinctive clay bluffs along this stretch of coast. New York State has one of the largest groupings of drumlins found anywhere in the world, with over ten thousand tallied. They are a ubiquitous landform throughout much of Wayne County. If you look closely at them, you'll see some variation in their shapes. Recent studies suggest that our drumlins were created over a relatively brief period of a few hundred years near the end of the Ice Age. When the glacier began to melt, it developed "ice streams." These were areas of rapid ice movement within the glacier. Meltwater at the base of the ice may have lubricated and hastened the speed of these "rivers" of ice. As they passed over deposits of till that had been left by previous glaciers, they formed the drumlins. Faster-moving ice probably created more elongated, stretched-out hills.

Layered limestone makes up much of the northeastern shoreline of Lake Ontario in the Henderson–Sacket's Harbor area. *Author collection.*

Drumlin end eroded by wave action of the lake. *Photo by Chris Gateley.*

Along the shore between Oswego and Sodus, where a number of drumlin ends are being eroded away by runoff and wave action, geologists can study the interior structure to get clues about the events of the Ice Age. Some of the bluffs, including Sitts Bluff and Chimney Bluff, both in state parks, show considerable variability in their sand and clay; distinct layers give a faintly banded look to the bluff face. Some of the bluffs have a sandier upper layer. Here you are most likely to see the holes created by nesting bank swallows and Kingfishers. Below that layer are other, more clay-rich deposits. Areas made up of thin layers of clay that resemble "varves" may appear, indicating that this part of the drumlin was formed under water as a lake bed where silt was deposited during runoff events in still waters. At least three different colors of clay were obvious as of this writing in a lakeshore bluff near my house. Yellow, reddish and "blue" clay were all visible in various parts of the cutaway drumlin ends.

These differences in sediment and layering suggest a complicated process of original deposition. Some observers have interpreted this sequence of beds

McIntyre Bluff at the Sterling Nature Center shows a layer of lighter-colored, higher sand content where the birds have excavated nest holes. *Photo by Susan P. Gateley.*

as evidence of more than one glacial advance and retreat across the area. The highly sculptured spires and ridges of Chimney Bluffs State Park and Sitts Bluff on the east side of Fair Haven Beach State Park show dramatically the uneven erosion of more resistant clays and more easily eroded sandier sediment, suggesting a complicated process of original deposition.

So, rather than a homogeneous dump, the drumlins are now thought to have been preexisting forms left by earlier Ice Ages before the last glacier gave them their current shapes.

While the thought of a mass of ice a thousand feet thick lying over where my house and computer now exist strikes me as pretty grim, people adapted to and even thrived during the Ice Age. It has even been suggested that we may owe the beginnings of "civilization" to ice. The theory goes that people banded together and worked cooperatively to survive the brutal conditions of the Ice Age, advancing their technology to do so. While this may be tough to prove, there is another benefit of the Ice Age that seems pretty well documented: its impact on soil fertility.

As the glacier pushed its vast weight across the land, it ground rocks into fragments and dust, releasing minerals to the soil. These minerals contribute to what the author of 1902's *Geography of New York State* calls our "strong soils." Recently glaciated, mineral-rich soils are far more productive than are the leached-out, nutrient-poor soils of the southern United States and the tropics. Most of today's gravel and sand pits, occasional bogs and our big swamps like the Montezuma marshes, also owe their existence to the Ice Age and the shallow glacial lakes that were formed immediately after its retreat. And today, when you hit that hard head in the north lawn with the mower, you can thank the glacier for it.

2

THE EUROPEANS ARRIVE

The French first made their way up the St. Lawrence River in 1534. They sought a water passage through North America that would provide a route to the riches of Cathay. Instead of Oriental silks and gold, however, they found forests, rivers and lakes filled with a variety and abundance of life that is almost unbelievable today. Trees of great size and beauty made up "the finest forests imaginable" along the lakeshore, according to one traveler, who wrote of pines, firs and cedars "of a height and thickness perfectly astonishing" in "forests as ancient as the world," where "trees hide their tops in the clouds." In this pre-settlement world, flocks of birds blackened the skies, and rivers and lakes swarmed with fish. The French also found people, and it wasn't long before they got involved in an unfortunate squabble between the related but hostile tribes of the Iroquois and the Huron that had long-lasting impacts on North American history.

It's thought that the region's indigenous residents came into the area as a single group perhaps a century or so before the French arrival, probably pushing other clans out in order to take up residence. Huron and Iroquois language and customs were similar, but the formerly united tribes had been at odds for some time before European contact. In 1609, Samuel de Champlain sided with the Huron in a military skirmish against the Iroquois at a location near Lake Champlain that had political repercussions for centuries to come. You can learn about that event and its eventual effects on Lake Ontario's ecology in various regional history books, but we will stick to the primal natural history of our lake for now.

Plaque at the Old Mill Inn, Toronto, showing the explorer Etienne Brule in his native mode. *Wikipedia*.

The woodlands that surrounded the lake were part of a vast, predominantly hardwood forest that originally stretched from the East Coast to the Mississippi River. The dense canopy of oak, chestnut, beech, maple and elm shaded the forest floor and reduced undergrowth in many areas along the lakeshore. Where trees had been blown down or burned up, however, vines and young growth crowded the openings, and the occasional windfall jumbles of tree trunks and limbs challenged early travelers. Water routes like the sixteenth-century superhighway of the Great Lakes were almost always preferred to bushwhacking through the wilderness.

Though the road to Cathay's riches proved an illusion for over a century, the French were quick to recognize that the timber and plants of the forest and the animals and fishes of New France were treasures in their own right. Historic accounts detail white pines over 250 feet tall with trunks 7 feet in diameter. Such trees were highly valued as timber for masts for cargo and navy ships and were of great strategic value. And within a few years of Jacques Cartier's first foray up the river as far as Montreal, the rush was on for the dense fine fur of the beaver and the legendary healing powers of the ginsang (mandrake) root.

Etienne Brule was the first White man to view the expanses of Lake Ontario. Born in France around 1592, he left for Canada as a teenager and at the direction of Champlain went to live with the Hurons to learn their language and customs and to explore the general lay of the land. He promptly went native, embracing the indigenous tribes' customs and their women with enthusiasm. He explored as far west as Lake Superior and south into Pennsylvania and beyond to the Chesapeake Bay. He probably saw Lake Ontario for the first time during a scouting expedition in 1615.

What the French Found

Early accounts of the land through which Brule traveled describe a great bounty of game for the hungry hunter. "Roe deer" (today known as white-tailed deer), "elk" (moose), bear and great numbers of waterfowl abounded. Flocks of "bustards" (possibly geese), ducks and "pheasants" (possibly grouse or partridge), as well as schools of fish, supplied food for early explorers and settlers.

One who came to the New World and saw Lake Ontario and its coasts in pre-settlement times was Pierre François Xavier de Charlevoix, who arrived about a century after Brule. Charlevoix had "an eager curiosity concerning life" that comes through vividly in his writing. The indigenous people's awareness of the region's botany and animal life was carefully recorded by Charlevoix and other early Jesuit missionaries; at that time, knowledge of the natural environment was fundamental to human survival and the eventual development and success of the New World settlements.

Voltaire, who in his student days knew Charlevoix, called him "a most veracious man." Charlevoix, of distinguished ancestry, began his training as a Jesuit scholar around the age of sixteen. He was sent in 1705 to New France to teach in a Jesuit college in Quebec. In 1720, he was sent west into the little-known interior of New France to investigate rumors of a western sea that separated New France from the Orient and to gather information in support of French expansionist ambitions in the New World. He never made it to the Pacific Coast, but he did leave us a detailed and perceptive account of the Great Lakes country through which he passed. He had a keen interest in the resources of the still largely unknown region. His notes on botany and medical herbs, wildlife, the customs of the native peoples and hunting and fishing paint a vivid portrait of a long-vanished world. He was a careful observer of the region's geography and items of potential commerce. Historians recognize the accuracy of his descriptions and have characterized his work as "one of the most important journals of North American historical literature." While traveling Lake Ontario's shore, he described the occurrence of seiches that caused fluctuations and currents in creek mouths and pondered the source of these "intermitting motions." He also accurately observed the formation and periodic opening of the barrier bars across the lake's south shore bays and rivers, and he noted how the lake's lingering chill slowed the onset of spring during his canoe journey in May along the south shore. More than once he praised the area's great beauty, with its lake waters "as clear as that of the purest fountain."

The great blue heron may have been the "gray crane" described by Charlevoix. *Photo by Susan P. Gateley.*

Charlevoix also described the region's vast multitudes of waterfowl, including the wood duck, "most delicate of eating" with its "varigated and brilliant plumage." He called these small ducks "bough wild ducks," from their habit of perching on the boughs of trees. There were also, he recorded, two kinds of "cranes," one white and one gray, that made "excellent soop."

In the days before the neighborhood supermarket, everyone ate local. In this new land and climate, where French agricultural methods remained unproven and winter famine was far from rare, the variety and availability of food was a constant topic in his and in other early travelers' dispatches.

The indigenous Haudenosaunee and the neighboring Huron on the lake's north shore cultivated a number of crops in clearings around their villages. Their native foods included corn, several types of beans used both as green and dried vegetables and at least two kinds of squash, one of which was usually boiled or roasted under the ashes of their fires. They also grew the native sunflower known to us as the Jerusalem artichoke.

Charlevoix called it the soleil. The villagers cultivated another plant that Charlevoix described as one that sprouted like asparagus and grew to a height of about three feet. This plant, he wrote, produced pods filled with a fine fluffy sort of cotton and at its top grew "several tufts of flowers. In the morning before the dew has fallen off they shake the flowers and there falls from it with the humidity a kind of honey which by boiling is reduced to a kind of sugar." This surely is a description of the milkweed plant with its edible broccoli like flower buds and fragrant blossoms. He recorded that the woodlands also supplied wild strawberries, raspberries, blueberries and three types of currents.

Fish, a major part of the indigenous diet, were vital to the French as well. Charlevoix wrote, "The rivers of this land were perhaps the most plentifully stocked with fish in the whole world." Each summer, the Haudenosaunee set up seasonal camps by the lake to exploit the vast runs of salmon, trout, sturgeon, perch and bullhead and to harvest the all-important eel—"a manna exceeding all belief," as another Jesuit observer wrote. The Jesuit missionary, Father Dablon, whose travels preceded Charlevoix by about seventy years, described fish runs in a river at the east end of the lake.

> In the spring as soon as the snows melt it is full of gold-colored fish; next come carp, and finally achigen. The latter is a flat fish half a foot long and of very fine flavor. Then comes the brill and at the end of May, when strawberries are ripe, sturgeon are killed with hatchets. All the rest of the year until winter, the salmon furnishes food.... We made our bed last night

The soleil, also called the sun root, Jerusalem artichoke and earth apple, has an edible tuber-like root used by indigenous folk of the lakeshore region. *Photo by Susan P. Gateley.*

on the shore of a lake where the natives toward the end of winter, break the ice and catch fish, or rather draw them up by the bucketful.

Possibly the gold-colored early running fish were yellow perch, while the "carp" were probably suckers, carp not being introduced into Lake Ontario from Europe until many years later. The "flat" achigan were probably bullheads, but "brill" stumps me. Perhaps this was the fish we call the walleye or possibly the pickerel.

The eel was one of the most important foods of the Haudenosaunee. The Onondaga Nation includes an eel clan among its five traditional kinship groups. The oily flesh of the eel made it well suited to smoking as a means of preservation for winter food stocks. The French, who knew the closely related European eel from their homeland, were quick to appreciate tribal methods of fishing. The tribes built weirs of stone or brush to trap eels as they made their fall runs downstream. They also speared eels at night using torches set up in the bows of the canoe. Often, their torches were made of twisted birch bark that burned with a bright light, and fishermen also sometimes set up a piece of white birch bark behind the torch to help "reflect" its light outward. Charlevoix wrote of the eel, "The best way to eat them is to hang them up in a chimney and let them fry slowly in their skins which come off of themselves and let the oil run out."

The Europeans also salted eels for storage and barreled then up, and I've heard that the native people kept live eels in small containers for long periods in the winter. Today, the eel has all but vanished from Lake Ontario, having fallen victim to the turbines of the St. Lawrence Seaway's power dam. But efforts continue to bring back the fish that once may have constituted up to a third of the biomass of the lake's inshore shallows and bays.

The Beaver

Soon, Champlain and Brule were followed by trappers and traders, as well as by Jesuit missionaries, who left us descriptions of the region's early residents and their customs in regular annual reports between 1632 and 1673. These are preserved as *The Relations of New France*, since translated and placed online. These works, along with those of Charlevoix, paint a vivid picture of unspoiled bounty, great beauty and terrible hardship. Winters were particularly hard for European and native inhabitants alike. Charlevoix wrote: "I have never passed a winter in this country without seeing someone or other being carried to the hospital, who was obliged to have his legs or arms cut off on account of their being benumbed and frozen....The wind that blows from the west is intolerably piercing."

It's little wonder in this place of bitter winter weather that the fur trade built fortunes and initiated wars and strife across the Great Lakes country and Canada. And no creature suffered more slaughter from the trade than the thickly furred rodent known for its work ethic and engineering skills. In 1600, the busy brown beaver was ubiquitous across our area. Beavers created ponds and swamps on almost every stream and river in the Lake Ontario watershed and built their lodges and bankside tunnels on countless marshes by the lake. Beaver ponds were an important part of the region's ecology, contributing diversity in the form of numerous small sunlit wetlands amid the dense forest. These highly productive areas were rich in plant and animal life. Algae and diatoms provided the base of a food chain that culminated ultimately in moose, deer, otter and wolf. And beaver ponds contributed to those crystal-clear precolonial waters of the lake.

Beaver lodge in lakeshore marsh area of Fair Haven Beach State Park. *Photo by Susan P. Gateley.*

Rain that falls on the forested lands by the lake flows overland into a stream or soaks into the ground to sustain trees and vegetation or to ultimately replenish underlying aquifers. When in a stream, moving water carries soil particles with its flow, and the constant scour of the stream's current limits life to plants and animals that can stay put in the current. But when a forest creek is blocked by a beaver dam, the impounded still waters soon warm in the sun and nourish abundant plant life. Pond water also percolates downward, being filtered and cleansed on its way to underlying aquifers. Ultimately, the wetland contribution raises the water table to create springs that may supply cool, shaded woodland streams with year-round flow. The thousands of beaver ponds that once spotted the lake's watershed contributed greatly to its overall health and diversity of life.

Felt hats became fashionable among European counts and princes by the late 1500s. And no fur made better felt than the fluffy, soft undercoat of the beaver. Europe's beaver population had been pretty well trapped out by the time French traders moved inland from the saltwater coasts of North America to establish posts along the St. Lawrence. Here they found fresh stocks of fur bearers and native people willing to trap them in exchange for steel. Cookware, knives, guns and alcohol changed the world of the Huron.

So did disease. Even so, it didn't take long for native hunters to clean out Lake Ontario's population of beavers. The fur traders then moved west and north, cleaning out the valuable rodents as they went. By the 1890s, the beaver was mere memory on our shores. As beaver ponds drained to become meadows and brush and the lakeshore forests were cleared by European settlers, springs dried up and many small streams became intermittent or too warm and sluggish for native trout and young salmon to survive in.

Once the Jay Treaty settled the boundary between the United States and Canada and the British vacated Forts Niagara and Oswego around 1796, settlement began, followed by forest clearing and millpond construction to provide hydropower from tributary streams and rivers. This action further degraded the lake's watershed even as salmon, sturgeon and other fish were blocked from spawning grounds. Waste from tanneries and, a few years later, pollution from various factories further degraded tributaries and bays. As the web of life began to fray, the stage was set for a whole series of nonhuman immigrant arrivals (see chapter 11). By 1880, three-quarters of New York State's primal forests were gone, transformed into pasture and farm fields. Ironically, the arrival of fossil fuel–powered farm equipment along with the coal-powered transcontinental railroad proved to be a boon to the region's forests. Pasturage for draft animals was no longer needed; bigger, better, less stony farm fields out west beckoned. Large areas of the state that were marginal for farming were abandoned. Today, woodlands of oak, maple, birch and beech make up a respectable second growth of trees on many properties within the lake's watershed. And with the return of alder, willow and other trees, the beaver, New York State's "official mammal," has also made a comeback.

3

SEASONS ON THE LAKE

SPRING

Lake Ontario is so large that it makes its own weather. Its vast volume of water is slow to warm in the spring and slow to give up summer's heat each fall. This thermal "inertia" moderates climate extremes within several miles of its shore year-round. In the winter, minimum temperatures average ten degrees higher near the lake, putting the south shore in horticultural plant hardiness Zone 5. Ten miles to the south is considered to be Zone 4. Canada's Niagara Peninsula, surrounded by Lakes Erie and Ontario, is rated zone 7, one of the most temperate regions in all of eastern Canada. This climate moderation, along with the effects the lake has on daily weather, occurs because of the unique physical and chemical characteristics of water. Without water's chemical oddity, life on earth as we know it would not exist.

Water molecules in liquid phase are attracted to each other by hydrogen bonds. Because these weak chemical bonds absorb and release a lot of heat, large volumes of water act to moderate temperature extremes on nearby land. Hydrogen-bonded molecules also influence the density of water. When water freezes, its molecules form a crystalline structure. The orientation of the bonds between them causes the molecules to move farther apart as it solidifies, lowering water's density. So ice floats. Most liquids become denser when they solidify, but water is most dense at about four degrees Celsius (thirty-nine degrees Fahrenheit). If water behaved like most liquid compounds, lakes would freeze from the bottom up, and aquatic life in temperate regions would be very different and probably far less diverse.

Because water is most dense at four degrees Celsius, freshwater lakes in the north generally follow a seasonal pattern of circulation and stratification that profoundly affects the life within them. In spring and fall, when their waters become uniformly four degrees, the entire lake mixes, circulating nutrients from the bottom and oxygen downward from the surface. But in winter and summer, lakes stratify. The periodic mixing makes the survival of diverse aquatic life possible. Without mixing, the bottom waters of lakes would become anaerobic as bacterial decay would use up all the oxygen.

Each winter, Lake Ontario stratifies with less dense ice or very cold water at its surface. Because of wave action, it's rare for the entire lake to freeze over. With denser four-degree water below the ice, the lake stratifies. However, when the strong sunlight of March begins to warm the icy surface, that water warms, melts and becomes heavier. Now that water sinks. As the stratification breaks down, the entire lake's volume mixes in what limnologists call the spring turnover. This oxygenates the entire lake and also brings nutrients up to the sunlit surface. The mixing goes on for a month or more on Lake Ontario.

When the water that has been near the bottom mixes with surface water, one-celled algae and diatoms that spent the cold, dark winter as inert resting "spores" react to the abrupt increase in light energy and nutrients. The result is a "bloom" of planktonic plant life soon followed by a rapid increase in algae-eating zooplankton. Diatoms are a major part of this spring bloom on the open lake. Diatoms are microscopic, single-celled plants found in fresh water and salt water alike. They are distinguished from other algae by a glasslike silicon cell covering, often etched with intricate markings. These all-but-invisible but hugely abundant plants are believed to produce up to half of our planet's global supply of oxygen. Oil-rich and nutritious, diatoms are an ideal food for the freshwater copepods and water fleas that in turn are key food items for the lake's larval fishes. By May or June, as numerous species of fish move inshore into the warmer, nutrient-rich sunlit waters to spawn, the open lake, like the newly leafed-out forests on shore, has become a veritable chlorophyll factory with abundant food for the newly hatched fishes.

As the lake continues to warm, its surface water becomes less dense. Eventually, it stratifies again, this time with a layer of warmer water above and colder, denser water in its depths. Separating the two is a narrow region of rapid temperature change called the thermocline. This feature is of great interest to Lake Ontario anglers, as their quarry, the salmon and trout, often hang around just below the thermocline in cool water. When

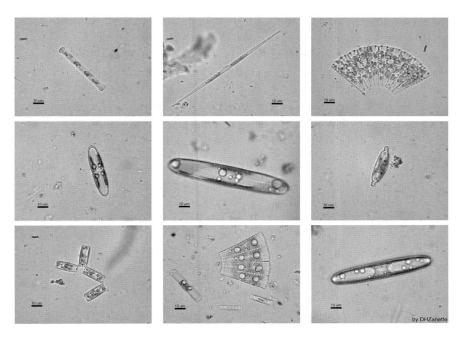

Various species of diatoms, with their intricately etched silicon shells, are an important part of the base of Lake Ontario's food chain. *Wikipedia.*

it's dinner time, the fish make brief forays up into the warmer sunlit waters to feed on bait fish that in turn are feeding on zooplankton.

In the spring, as stratification begins, a sharp boundary between warm and cold water develops along the shore. This "front," called the thermal bar, between warm and cold, features a current of sinking water that acts as a physical barrier to separate the inshore and offshore waters. This is of importance to science, fish, anglers, zooplankton and human water drinkers, because the nearshore water tends to trap and concentrate nutrients and pollutants from runoff. For this reason, fishermen, public-health workers and the folks that run water and sewer plants along the south shore like to keep informed as to its extent. The thermal bar can also influence the distribution of toxic algae blooms by concentrating phosphates from sewage and farm-field run off and keeping them near shore.

One study of Lake Superior estimated that perhaps 70 percent of the total dissolved solids input (and associated pollutants) enters the lake during spring runoff. If it's all concentrated inshore by the thermal bar, the implications for water quality are obvious. Diatoms and zooplankton

Salmon fishermen seek out the thermocline for trophy catches. *Photo from Werner Stenger.*

tend to concentrate along the thermal bar, as do bait fish and, ultimately, all of those hungry, big silver salmon.

Though I have no science to back it up, as a sailor, I wonder if the thermal bar can also sometimes influence the wind. More than once in late spring, I've seen a sudden shift in wind speed and/or direction, from brisk southerly to a lighter northeaster, along with a temperature drop after reaching the colder lake waters offshore when I travel to or from Canada with my boat. Perhaps the layer of cold, dense air over the still-frigid early summer lake sometimes blocks southerly winds. A hot-air balloonist website states that winds may be light and blow from a completely different direction from prevailing weather system winds within such an inversion. Cold surface water offshore also can act as a fog generator, and early June can be a foggy time on the lake.

The lake often stratifies quite quickly in the summer. In June, more than once on a sunny, seventy-degree day with a south wind, I've headed to Canada aboard my sailboat. Five or six miles offshore, the air temperature drops into the fifties. For the next several hours of motoring or sailing through forty-degree water, the winter hat, scarf, gloves and every sweater available are in service. While people onshore are sunbathing on the beach in the hot June sun, we shiver and stamp our feet and try to warm up with hot soup or coffee during clammy lake crossings. I've resorted to a blanket over my legs as I sit at the tiller. Yet, just a week later, on our return trip across the lake, stratification is complete, and a light sweater or a long-sleeved shirt is all the helmsman needs while sailing on sunlit waters.

During trips to the nearby beach with my family back in the 1950s, we sometimes encountered very clear, very icy water on a hot August day. This, I was informed, was caused when the lake "turned over." Nowadays, we speak of upwellings of cold water to explain the same event. Upwellings and a thirty-degree drop can make swimming a challenge. They usually occur after a day or two of strong offshore winds. These push the warm surface water offshore, allowing denser cold water to rise to the surface. Usually, the nice, warm, seventy-five-degree water returns within a few days as the "new" water mixes and warms. Often, fish are attracted to the "edge" between this warm and cold water, so anglers in search of salmon study satellite maps and other sources for information on upwellings and surface current flows.

Seasonal Lake Effects Ashore

Because of the lake's year-round climate moderation, New York is second only to Washington State in apple production. The lake's slow warming delays spring's arrival to nearby gardens and orchards, and the effect is especially strong along the lake's south shore, thanks to lake breezes that often set up here on sunny spring afternoons. These chilly winds delay spring fruit blossoms a week or more, making them less likely to be damaged by frost during their tender bud and flower stages. In the fall, cold northerly winds are moderated by heat retained in the lake, reducing the chance of early frost near shore. And some types of fruit trees respond poorly to temperatures over eighty-five degrees Fahrenheit, so the cooling lake breezes of summer further favor production. The lake's cooler surface also helps reduce the frequency of severe summer thunderstorms and hail that can be so devastating to fruit crops.

The European settlers who came to the area were quick to recognize this localized moderation, which also established Rochester as a major nineteenth-century nursery area for fruit and ornamental trees. At one time, the Ellwanger Barry nursery was one of the largest in the United States. Established in 1838, the nursery and its five hundred acres of stock were described in the 1850s by Rochester historian Henry O'Reilly as

> *probably the most extensive Nursery in the world.... The Fruit Department occupies 350 acres, in about the following proportion of the different kinds: Standard pears, 69 acres; dwarf do., 57 acres; standard apples, 72 acres; dwarf do., 31 acres; standard and dwarf cherries, 25 acres; standard and dwarf plums, 20 acres; and 82 acres of other fruit trees, seedling stocks, &c.*

Today, the one-time nursery grounds make up part of Rochester's Highland Park, and the lakeshore region continues to produce millions of bushels of apples, plus cherries, peaches and plums each year.

Apple orchards near the lakeshore are protected from late frosts by cool spring breezes off the lake. *Photo by Susan P. Gateley.*

Warm air and cold water in the spring also work together to sometimes produce mirages out over the lake. They typically occur on a bright, sunny afternoon of light wind and cold water. Last spring, we went off for a few hours of sailing, heading north toward open water. When we turned back to sail home, the land before us transformed into something like a fantastic, transplanted shoreline version of Monument Valley. Distant, gigantic, flat-topped mesas and huge buttes of tawny brown and dark green now appeared to loom hundreds of feet in the air. A few isolated spires and columns also appeared, and the more distant headlands showed a distinct horizontal dark line like a layer of smoke trailing off over the water from the top of the mountainous horizon. Occasionally, as I studied this improbable shore, a little piece of a mesa top would detach itself and float up to dwindle away. The whole thing kept changing, but so slow and subtle were the shifts that it was almost impossible to track them. It was as if the front range of the Rockies had suddenly erupted before us.

Some mirages show multiple images inverted or compressed or otherwise distorted hanging over the water. These are caused by the presence of several layers of air of different temperatures. The images are sensitive to the height of the observer, and by climbing up onto the cabin top of the

Today, growers increasingly use intensive trellis systems for higher yields of apples with less labor costs. *Photo by Susan P. Gateley.*

Typical spring "looming" mirage of land (*left*), and inverted and right-side-up images stacked on top of one another as a Fata Morgana mirage. *Photo by Susan P. Gateley.*

boat or to the highest point on a beach, you can get a different mirage than if you stay a few feet lower.

Most springtime Lake Ontario mirages are the superior type, in which something below the horizon appears to float above it. You need a temperature difference of ten to twenty degrees Fahrenheit to see a mirage. You are most likely to see a them on days of light wind that won't stir up and mix the atmosphere near the lake surface.

Spring Bird Life by the Lake

Each spring for a thousand years, warm winds from the south bring birds to our shores. Sometimes in late April, sometimes in May, unseen in the dark night sky, they come. Warblers, vireos, grosbeaks, orioles and other small songbirds fly north. They navigate by the stars and possibly by other clues such as changes in the magnetic field as they fly. Exactly how they move hundreds or thousands of miles to return to their birthplaces remains a mystery. Often, when they reach the shore of Lake Ontario, they pause in their long journey from Central or South America to rest and feed for a day in the undeveloped woodlands and brushy overgrown areas before continuing on across the water the next night. Because the coast is a vital rest stop for the little travelers, the land within a half mile of the lake has been recognized as an "Important Birding Area" by ornithological organizations; seasonal observatories are set up during migration at Braddock's Bay and Derby Hill. Often, the small birds' arrival coincides with the first really massive midge hatches of the spring, providing the migrants with abundant food.

Some bird species migrate by day and follow the coast rather than going straight across the lake. Big birds like hawks and eagles especially are easily seen as they fly along the shoreline and then turn north at each end of the lake. These soaring birds depend on the rising air of thermals for lift and so are reluctant to cross the cool waters offshore with their dense "sinking" air. In March and April, tens of thousands of vultures and raptors flow silently along the lakeshore. The observatories at Braddocks Bay and Derby Hill maintain hawk watches and post counts and species seen on their websites. Derby Hill, fifteen miles east of Oswego, is recognized as one of the best places to see spring raptor migrations. But only if you look up.

The most spectacular aggregations of soaring birds occur when south winds push them north against the lake. Then the daily soaring bird counts run into the thousands. On such a day I once watched a "kettle" of several hundred hawks and eagles swirling overhead as they rode the wind ahead of an approaching rain squall. I only happened to see the spectacular aggregation of birds high overhead looking like a swarm of midges because I was sanding the topsides of my wooden boat and looked up at the next plank of its hull.

During their migration, the tiny, colorful songbirds known as warblers seriously test amateur bird-watchers' observation skills. These little snippets of life often flit around high overhead in the just-leafed-out forest canopy as they forage and defy all but the quickest eye. Good places to seek them and other spring bird travelers include the thickets and trees of Webster Park and Gosnells's Big Woods in Monroe County, the Sterling Nature Center in Cayuga County, the various Lakeshore Wildlife Management Areas of Wayne County and the forested parts of Derby Hill.

If possible, take an experienced bird-watcher with you who can identify them by their calls and songs. Warblers are a challenge, especially for those of us who are not highly skilled bird-watchers. But if you do actually manage to identify one of these brightly colored, tiny songsters, it's intensely satisfying. You really earn an identification of a warbler as the tiny birds flit around constantly, often forty feet up in the top of a tree. There's a reason experienced bird-watchers identify many by their calls and songs.

They and dozens of other songbirds arrive just as the trees leaf out, often when some of the season's early and most massive aquatic midge hatches are occurring along the coast. These vast aggregations of harmless nonbiting flies, many of them of the family Chironomidae, are a vital part of both aquatic and terrestrial food webs. The larval stages live on the bottom or on aquatic vegetation in lakes and ponds. Fish of many types, including minnows, trout, sculpins and Great Lakes sturgeon, feed on them. Along the shore, adult midges are an important food source to spring migrant birds who pause along the forested areas of the Great Lakes to rest before heading north.

The numbers of these insects are simply unimaginable. Some live on the bottom hundreds of feet down as aquatic larvae feeding on detritus and bacteria in the black depths of the lake. Some live near shore in the sunlit shallows and feed on one-celled algae. They are worldwide in distribution. As adults, some feed on nectar or pollen. Some don't feed at all.

The swarms are first formed by male midges. They apparently use sound to find one another and organize into a swarm. The male midges' feathery antennae are designed to pick up the high-frequency noise of their millions

Huge swarms of midges emerge on calm spring days, sometimes clogging every web on the lakeshore. *Photo by Susan P. Gateley.*

of beating wings. One internet article says it takes ten midges to form a self-organized swarm. Then the females fly through and pick one out for their betrothed. Off they go as a couple to make more midges. Somehow, she then gets back to the lake to drop her eggs. How they all decide to emerge at once for the big dance is a mystery and a marvel. Some say it's the phases of the moon. I once saw hundreds of big midges popping out of the calm water around my boat during the day. Perhaps different midges use different signals to coordinate the party.

Hungry spring bird travelers make good use of the midges even as they glean for other insects among the forest canopy or leaf litter. I have learned from a sharp-eyed bird-watcher friend that often the best way to see a warbler is to stand still. Sometimes, the little bird will come to you as it feeds. It's a lot easier to identify these fast-moving bits of color if they're five or ten feet away. Standing still also fits in with good birding etiquette. While bird-watching would seem to be a benign activity, your presence can impact birds adversely. Each time a bird has to avoid you by flying away, it's not spending time foraging and fueling up for the next leg of its journey north.

One spring visitor to the lake that I always look for is the loon. They aren't common here except during migration, and I don't know of any summer breeding on the south shore, though I have seen loon pairs and babies being carried aboard their mothers' backs on the Canadian side of the lake. During spring and fall migration, you may see them on the bays, and you may hear that haunting, drawn-out call used by a pair to locate each other. It's something wonderous on a calm day or evening by the lake.

Another spring bird whose wild, piercing cries aloft are a welcome sign of warmer days to come is the ring-billed gull, whose flocks appear on and near the lake early in the spring. Most of these small gulls with their distinctively marked bills and yellowish feet spend the winter in the south. They begin appearing in the farm fields and on the waters of the lake in March and April. Many of the adult birds gather in island breeding colonies in the Kingston- Henderson Harbor area to raise their young. After the young fledge along about August, they then show up again on fields, docks and parking lots.

Like the larger herring gull, these ubiquitous little hustlers are as tough as they come and can thrive "on almost any available source of nutrition," as the bird book puts it. Not for nothing are they called flying rats by some boat

Midges on the wing at dusk. Note the faint, smoke-like smudge beside the tree. *Photo by Susan P. Gateley.*

The ring-billed gull is often associated with fresh water in summer, while many Lake Ontario birds winter on the Gulf Coast. *Photo by Susan P. Gateley.*

owners tired of cleaning up after them. But they enliven the lakefront with their acrobatic flight and noisy squabbles in restaurant parking lots. They do eat fish as well as French fries, waste corn, cherries and earthworms, among other things. I once saw a considerable number of them feeding on the wing on insects like swallows over a lakeshore marsh. I also enjoy watching them interact as they perch in a line on the channel jetty. They space themselves out in a very uniform pattern of social distancing here, and if someone intrudes on another's space, the bird lets the offender and everyone else around know it with a series of loud shrieks and calls.

SPRING BIRD COURTSHIP

Spring bird behaviors include courtship and parenting. Among the waterfowl on bays and lakeshore marshes, these activities can be very entertaining. One easily observed spring courtship ritual is that of the mute swan, a recent immigrant considered an "invasive" species that made its way to Lake Ontario shortly after being introduced to ponds and creeks of estates in the Hudson River and New York City areas. Thousands of these Eurasian birds have adapted to our marshes and wetlands and are now a common sight (and hazard) to canoeists and kayakers. Mute swans are considered detrimental to the health and biodiversity of our region's marshes, as the aggressive, powerful birds readily out-compete native waterfowl for food and nest sites. But without a doubt, these pushy pests are entertaining to watch. Just don't get close to a couple with babies if you're in an easily capsizeable boat, as the protective male may launch a ferocious attack. (Swan attacks on small, tippy boats in cold water have drowned more than one kayaker or canoeist.)

Mute swans are far from mute and make a variety of grunts and whinnies. They also use a lot of dramatic body language to communicate with one another. Watch out if you see a bird raise its wings and puff up in a posture called busking. The bird means business and wants you gone. They are extremely territorial when they are guarding small cygnets and often skirmish with one another over rights to a bit of water in the nesting season. When one male runs off a rival, he typically charges over the water, wings flapping and big feet slapping the surface loudly. If you see a pair of birds sitting breast to breast on the water with their heads held high and neck feathers

Male swans usually station themselves in a conspicuous place near the nest as guardians. Give them plenty of space, as they can be very aggressive. *Photo by Susan P. Gateley*.

fluffed up, this is an expression of friendship or love. Sometimes, the pair will make that classic swan heart shape with their arched necks as they touch bills. Head bobbing and dipping is a form of mutual acknowledgement and possibly respect. And just before mating, male and female sometimes twine their necks together in a graceful display of mutual affection. (Did swans inspire the term *necking* for teen activity in a car's back seat?) Since the big, showy birds are probably here to stay, I suppose it makes sense to enjoy the show and be glad you're not a Canada goose.

FISH MIGRATIONS

Though they aren't as easy to observe as migrating birds, spring fish movements also are part of the rhythm of the lake's changing seasons. As the water warms, a number of fish species move inshore into the productive, sunlit shallows of bay and lake alike to spawn. Some fish, including various sucker species, perch and spring-spawning trout, move into rivers and creeks to seek out gravel bottom and riffles for their eggs. Carp—big, brown and wary but great fun to watch—move into the cattails and weedy backwaters to flail and thrash, broadcasting their adhesive eggs, which settle on and stick to aquatic vegetation. Fish watchers can easily observe bass and sunfish nests in protected clear shallows in May and early June. The parent fish use their fins to sweep silt off the pebbly bottom, so the circular nests show up as lighter areas and are quite conspicuous in two to four feet of water. Sunfish and bass parents guard their eggs, as do bullheads and the bowfin, a somewhat secretive but fairly common fish of weedy shallows. Alas, more than once I've seen a parent sunny chase off a pesky goby, only to have two or three more of the little opportunists move in to snatch a quick lunch of sunfish eggs.

Gobies spend the winter in the lake's deeper waters before moving back inshore for the summer. The round goby is a newcomer to Lake Ontario. Like the zebra mussel, the fishhook water flea and more than one hundred other alien animals and plants, it arrived in the Great Lakes via ship ballast water. Native to the Black and Caspian Seas, the first ones started to show up in Lake Ontario in the mid-1990s. Gobies don't get big enough to interest human anglers, six inches being about the biggest I've seen, however, they are very popular items on the menu of various Lake Ontario fish eaters, including the smallmouth bass and various fish-eating

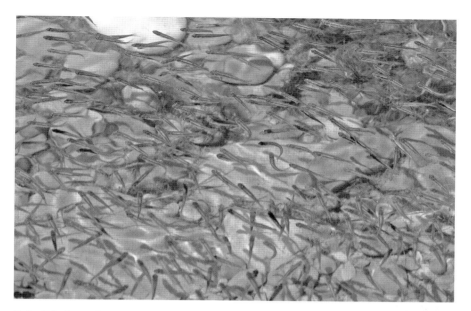

Baby fish depend on the zooplankton of the lake's sheltered sunlit shallows. *Photo by Susan P. Gately.*

birds. They are extremely abundant at times. Every other rock in the lake's pebbly shallows sometimes seems to have a two- to three-inch goby sitting on it on calm days. (See chapter 11 for more on the goby and its role in toxic botulism outbreaks.)

As the inshore waters warm in late April and May, schools of alewife seek the sunlit shallows to spawn. They also enter bays and open marsh areas. Looking down on the lake on clear, calm days from an elevated vantage point, you can sometimes see the glint of silver as sunlight strikes the sides of fish in a school a few feet offshore, and they often break the surface briefly. Alewife mainly spawn at night. You may then hear them swishing around in their circling dances of procreation in the weedy shallows. They also run up some of the lake's tributary streams, just as their ancestors once swarmed into East Coast creeks and rivers. Though today's fish runs lack the abundance and variety of migrations two hundred years ago, the age-old patterns continue if you know when and where to seek them.

4

SEASONS ON THE LAKE

TWO MONTHS OF SUMMER FOLLOWED BY FALL

Summer days and warm surface water bring out human lake users. Swim beaches attract crowds of sun lovers, and Jet Skis whine and high-powered, offshore speedboats thunder over the water on calm days. Salmon fishermen roar up to ten miles offshore with their big boats to fish the thermocline, while bass fishing reigns supreme close to land and in the bays. Crews of wind-driven craft often enjoy cool, gentle onshore breezes on sunny days, though localized thermal winds can be fickle and hard to predict along the south shore of the lake. As in the spring, the lake breeze is driven by the temperature difference between land and water. When the afternoon sun heats the shore, air over it rises, and heavier, cooler air from the lake flows in under it. The effect usually only reaches a few miles inland on the south shore, but it can be quite dramatic. Many times while running errands inland along Ridge Road, I've observed flags showing a grand southerly sailing wind of ten to fifteen miles an hour. However, on reaching home a half mile from the lake, I'm greeted by limp flags and nary a wiggle in the leaves as the northerly onshore breeze cancels out the southerly. But when we do get a light lake breeze on those hot, muggy July afternoons, it's a lifesaver, as it cools the day down ten degrees or more.

But it's a different story at the northeastern corner of the lake and in Canada, where the onshore wind reinforces prevailing summer southwesters. Here, Sackets and Henderson Harbor sailors may experience ten- to twenty-knot breezes while a "slick c'am" prevails off Oswego. The localized geographic enhancement of lake breezes has made the Canadian city of

Kingston a veritable powerhouse for competitive sailing. Many Olympic hopefuls have honed their skills with reliable afternoon winds on the choppy waters off its harbor. This paragraph was written on a June afternoon when the mirror-like waters of Little Sodus Bay were darkened by a few patches of ripples on a day of light and variable breezes. However, according to the internet, at the same time, Kingston had a sweet, steady onshore breeze blowing at ten knots.

The cool, dense air over the lake's colder waters also suppresses development of rising thermals and subsequent cloud buildup. On summer afternoons, the onshore lake breeze pushes cool, moist air inland, where it often meets with the warm south wind to form a convergence of contrasting air masses. This boundary is frequently marked by the development of a line of puffy cumulus clouds by midday even as the skies remain clear over the water. On hot, humid days, the clouds often continue to grow, so by late afternoon the sight of a bank of towering cumulus or even anvil-topped thunderheads to the south is common. Localized downpours and thunder often develop ten or twenty miles south of the lake in July and August while skies remain clear over the beach and lawns remain dry.

These sunny summer afternoons are a reverse of the lake-effect weather we experience in the fall and winter, when the clouds often hover over the lake and bring rain squalls and snow to the shore.

Banks of cumulous clouds form along the convergence areas ten to fifteen miles inland from the lake on many summer days. *Photo by Susan P. Gateley.*

I can't think of a better place to watch weather than on or beside the waters of a Great Lake. Lake Ontario's wide skies and distant horizons are a constantly changing panorama of cloud, light and shadow. On a recent summer sail, after I cleared the harbor channel and ventured out on the open lake, I observed a vast cloud bank extending east to west across the entire northern horizon. Silver and gray and snow-white cumulus loomed to Himalayan heights, a vaporous version of a snowcapped mountain range. During a three-hour sail, the cloud bank oozed southward, growing higher and darker and eventually becoming shrouded in gray status. This particular cold front gave plenty of warning, and by the time the wind shifted from southwest to north, I was safely ashore and still dry. Some days aren't so benign, though.

The sailor, like the pilot of a small airplane, keeps his eyes on the sky, for the lake can surprise even the experienced. The speed with which open water can kick up a four-foot sea during a summer squall continues to amaze the unwary, who "suddenly" find themselves in water too rough for comfort.

Wave action on the lake shapes its beaches and its relationship with those in the home-building business who would profit from its waters. Erosion, as we will see in chapter 6 on the natural history of our beaches, is a serious force for change when it comes to real estate appraisals of waterfront property. And the lake's waves have long influenced regional history in war and peace. Hundreds of wrecked wooden ships fell prey to the lake's fury, especially in the late fall. Overwhelmed by waves up to twenty feet high, they and their cargoes of coal, stone, salt or grain went to the bottom and remain in the dark stillness, preserved by the cold waters.

Unlike in the marine environment, sunken ships on the Great Lakes aren't subject to the action of marine borers, while the cold darkness of its bottom water slows chemical and biological decay. Because of this, some regions of our inland seas host virtual museums of sailing ships and early wooden steamers. There are tales of edible cheese brought to the surface in the early twentieth century by salvage divers from wrecks that had been sunk years before.

Two areas of Lake Ontario are known for their dozens of wooden shipwrecks. These maritime graveyards lie along the southern side of Prince Edward County to the northeastern portion of Canada's shoreline and the Mexico Bay area at the lake's east end. They support a modest underwater tourism industry of sport divers, and on Lake Ontario, a marine "sanctuary" area has been designated off of New York's shores to promote awareness of this unseen historical collection.

In 1980, Jacques Cousteau used his mini-sub to photograph the remains of two small ships dating to the War of 1812 at the lake's west end for *National Geographic* magazine. The two gunboats, *Hamilton* and *Scourge*, were overwhelmed by a sudden night squall and sunk by its fierce winds in August 1813. They are among the most famous wrecks on the lake bottom. *National Geographic* published photos of the expedition that showed skeletal remains on the lake bottom and a haunting image of one ship's figurehead, a carved likeness of Diana the Huntress.

Many sunken vessels took their crews and passengers with them, and today's divers generally consider shipwrecks with fatalities grave sites and behave accordingly, allowing the dead to lie in peace and privacy. They also follow strict protocols of leaving objects and souvenirs in place. Take only photos and leave only bubbles, is the mantra of current reputable underwater tour guides and dive-shop operators.

Fall's changeable weather and shortening days send many birds and some insect species south, even as they bring faster-moving weather systems and strong winds to the lake. When air masses of sharply differing temperatures

Dozens of wooden schooners lost during fall and winter gales lie on the bottom of the lake, preserved by its cold waters. *Author's collection.*

from the interior of Canada and the Gulf of Mexico clash over the Great Lakes, the resulting storms are intensified by energy released from the still relatively warm waters. Just as hurricanes are fed by warm surface ocean temperatures, the residual warmth in the Great Lakes in October and November helps create smaller-scale weather "bombs," fast-growing, intense storm systems like the November gale that sank the iron-ore freighter *Edmund Fitzgerald* on Lake Superior in 1975. When the gales of November blow, winds of hurricane force can raise waves of twenty feet or more on the open waters of Lake Ontario.

During the fall, the lake's warmth releases moisture to colder air, moving over it to form those "lake-effect clouds" and gloomy skies so familiar to south-shore residents. As August moves on into September, that heat energy sometimes causes localized rain squalls with gusty winds, showers and even waterspouts. I recall driving home on a frosty night some years ago with a full moon lighting the landscape in early October. While I cruised along Lake Road near Pultneyville, I watched distant heat lightning flickering almost constantly in a cloud bank over the lake. Yet the tops of those cumulus clouds were brightly lit by the moon as the skies inland were crystal clear.

At this time, too, the ephemeral funnel clouds of waterspouts sometimes reach down from the clouds to march across the lake. In late August 2020, an "outbreak" occurred over a four-day period over several of the Great Lakes. Observers logged dozens of reports of waterspouts with the International Center for Water Spout Research's website. The center takes reports from "citizen scientists" as part of its effort to improve forecasting of these short-lived but potentially damaging aquatic tornadoes. Some of the observers have posted fascinating videos of the waterspouts on the organization's Facebook page.

We were out with our twenty-three-foot sailboat during that period with chilly northerly winds pushing us back to our home port from Oswego when we saw a black cloud a mile or so to the leeward of us sprout a nascent waterspout. Within a minute or two, it had enlarged, eventually reaching downward toward the water to form a tapered shape. Luckily, it was moving away from us, and the cloud mass disintegrated as soon as it reached land. The whole process of formation and dissipation took place over just a few minutes.

Great Lakes waterspouts can generate seventy-mile-an-hour winds, more than enough to shred sails or dis-mast small boats. I heard of one making landfall at a shoreline campground near Fair Haven that picked up a trailer and moved it fifteen feet. Most waterspouts are short-lived, though some can

Lake-effect cumulous clouds off Oswego formed by cold air moving across the still-warm lake in late August. *Photo by Susan P. Gateley.*

Waterspouts, like this one seen during a sail on the lake, dissipate rapidly once they hit land. *Photo by Chris Gateley.*

last up to twenty minutes. They move along at perhaps ten to fifteen knots and so are of little danger to motorboats. The tendril-like funnel that a full-blown spout develops is not formed of water sucked up from the surface, though the spouts do kick up a spray at the water surface as they move along. Rather, the funnel is a "condensation" cloud caused by cooler temperatures associated with the vortex.

An October storm on Lake Ontario two centuries ago may well have determined the location of today's boundary between Canada and the United States. Some say it might have prevented America from annexing its northern neighbor. I have written at some length on this storm, which occurred during the War of 1812, in *Maritime Tales of Lake Ontario* (The History Press, 2012). Here is a short recap of the story.

Late in the summer of 1813, American forces mounted a two-pronged attack on the strategic city of Montreal. One force consisting of eight thousand men under the command of General James Wilkinson was to cross Lake Ontario and then move down the St. Lawrence to join a second army that had moved overland on the assault. The amphibious force set out late in the season from Oswego in a flotilla of open flat-bottomed bateaux and double-ended rowboats. Through a series of foul-ups and blunders, the flotilla did not begin to cross the lake until mid-October. They left in darkness with their small, low-sided open boats crammed with ammunition, ordnance, hospital stores and two months of provisions. At first, the winds were light and the water calm as the men rowed their heavy vessels north. But then, in the blackness, the winds began to rise. Soon, rain, sleet and wind arrived in a squall line that struck with savage force. Likely there were flashes of lightning and thunder rolled and boomed as the crews and passengers of the open boats bailed for their lives and scudded before the wind. Ultimately, many boats drove ashore upon the rocky beaches of Point Peninsula and supplies and wreckage were strewn for miles. Fifteen boats were smashed to fragments, while others were heavily damaged. Stores, supplies and the irreplaceable ammunition were scattered for miles along the shore or lost altogether. Even after the men found their way to land and set up camp, the bad weather continued, with ten inches of heavy, wet lake-effect snow covering the ground. Some of the men began to weaken from cold and hypothermia as they waited out the weather, huddled under the scant shelter of canvas tents. The force was delayed nearly two weeks by weather and the need to make repairs. When at last they made their way down the St. Lawrence and finally met the much smaller British and Canadian forces on November 11 at the Battle of

Crysler's Farm, they were quickly defeated. One military historian noted that a shortage of ammunition probably contributed greatly to the British victory at the battle that has been said to have saved Canada.

Fall Migrations

Except for flocks of geese and waterfowl, fall bird movements along the lake's south shore are generally not as noticeable as they are in the spring. Hawks take a different route in September and October, and the small songbirds "stack up" on the Canadian side as they move south and many of them cross the lake at night. And now and then, small flocks of shorebirds may pause to pick through the pebbles and sands of the late-summer beach before moving on.

Sometimes, though, you may be lucky enough to see an insect migration—that of the monarch butterfly. These tiny travelers begin drifting southwest in late August. If you are on the water and see one pass overhead on a bearing for Mexico, you know you've seen a migrant.

The sanderling appears on our beaches in late summer and breeds in the high Arctic. Some birds fly over six thousand miles to South America. *Photo by Susan P. Gateley.*

Monarchs from Canada often move along shorelines on both sides of the lake, though they will sometimes go straight across its open waters if they have a good tailwind. And like the autumn migrant birds, they may concentrate along the north side of the lake, waiting for that favoring tailwind. Many years ago, I spent a warm, sunny day on the Canadian island of Main Duck in early September when its fields of goldenrod were loaded with resting butterflies waiting for the south wind to die so they could continue their journey to central Mexico. On another occasion, also in September, I watched a steady stream of monarchs moving along an undeveloped, forested shoreline in ones and twos and tens. The constant trickle of westward-flying butterflies went on for hours, and at sunset, dozens of butterflies fluttered overhead, seeking shelter in the forest foliage to roost for the night.

Monarchs aren't the only insects that migrate south. Several species of dragonflies also migrate, including the green darner, common in our lakeshore marshes. And the painted lady butterfly is the champion insect migrant. These little butterflies with a two-inch wingspan are much less conspicuous than the big black-and-orange monarch, but once in a while, conditions seem to favor big concentrations of migrants. On September

Painted ladies on sunflowers during a widespread and large movement of the butterflies reported in September 2017 across New York State. *Photo by Susan P. Gateley.*

23, 2017, I saw dozens in my overgrown yard a half mile inland from the lake fueling up on nectar from goldenrod and asters. Two days later, they had vanished.

Little is known about the fall movements of this common butterfly of global distribution, but undoubtedly, they, too, are influenced by the lake and its shorelines. Unlike the monarch, these little travelers don't concentrate in a single area for the winter. Rather, they remain dispersed and on the go, reproducing along the way and possibly ending up spread around the southwestern United States. One European study suggested that up to six generations made the round trip between northern Europe and tropical Africa over a distance of more than nine thousand miles.

5

SEASONS ON THE LAKE

WINTER WHITEOUTS AND ICE CASTLES

All too soon, fall days shorten, colorful foliage fades and the marshland flowers wither away. Winter arrives on the lake well before the December solstice as bitter winds blow lake-effect snows inland and, sometimes, winter thunder sounds out over the water. Lake-effect snow, like the fall rain squalls and late-summer waterspouts, is a product of the heat stored in the depths of Lake Ontario. The longer the distance the wind blows over the lake, the more moisture it picks up. When that moisture-laden air reaches shore, it's forced aloft, causing it to cool and dump the acquired moisture as snow. Because of its localized origins, the flakes are typically large and fluffy with a low moisture content. Shoveling a fresh lake snow on a still day is like tossing feathers around. But the same snow when driven by strong winds powders into hard-packed drifts and creates zero-visibility driving conditions.

At the lake's east end, a sparsely populated, elevated area called Tug Hill exaggerates the uplift of air that has traveled the entire length of the lake. The result is some of the heaviest snowfalls east of the Rocky Mountains. Snow accumulations of up to 6 inches an hour have been recorded, and more than one epic twenty-four-hour lake dump has resulted in six feet of new snow. Buffalo gets all the national attention compared to the small towns and sparsely populated countryside of "The Tug," but there's little doubt that this region of New York State is the champ when it comes to white stuff. During one ten-day period, 141 inches fell on the town of Redfield. Thirty-foot drifts have been whipped up, covering whole houses and collapsing barns in the past. In 2019, Redfield distinguished itself as the snowiest populated

Fluffy, low-moisture lake-effect snow piles up fast. *Photo by Susan P. Gateley.*

place in the nation when its residents had to shovel and snowblow more than twenty-five feet of fluffy lake snow from their driveways. A man who lived near Adams Center told me it wasn't unusual for the pile of snow under his deck on the north side of his house to persist into June.

Oswego and Syracuse also get their share of lake-effect snow. Often, however, it can be incredibly localized. Bands of snow sometimes only a few miles wide may form and persist for many hours. While your doorstep gets three feet of fluff, a neighbor five miles away enjoys sunshine and bright blue skies all day. Last winter, I watched a classic squall proceed down my residential village street. It advanced quite slowly inland, and for several minutes, two houses to the north, a wall of snow with hundred-yard visibility lingered. At my house, just a few flakes drifted down. The snow bands also move so that your location may go from clear blue skies and dry roads to intense blizzard-like, whiteout conditions in minutes. Then, with zero visibility, you drive along at a snail's pace trying to stay on the road by peering up at the cross arms of the utility poles that show dimly above the wind-driven powder around your car. A frequently told, possibly true story in various parts of the Great Lakes snowbelt has the narrator driving along at a crawl, following the dim taillights of a car just ahead in such a whiteout. Abruptly, the car stops, and the driver gets out. The motorist rolls his window down to ask, "Why did you stop?" and hears the reply, "Because I'm in my driveway now."

The weather service has collected extensive data to refine forecasting models for these intense, highly localized and sometimes life-threatening squalls. They are no fun to run into suddenly while traveling on Route 81 or other lakeshore highways. However, many forecasts still miss the mark each winter when it comes to predicting how much snow will fall at a given location.

Everyone around here probably has at least one good snow story, and several books have been written on lake snow. Wikipedia recalls the blizzard of '77, an event people still spoke of with awe twenty years later when I resided in Watertown in the 1990s. That storm hit the east end of the lake with literally tons of snow. Drifts of up to thirty feet clogged the roads, and U.S. Army and U.S. Marine troops from Camp Drum used half-tracks to get around on the hard-packed snow. At least one stranded car on a city street was "smushed" by an army vehicle, a neighbor recalled. The only way stranded people could be rescued was by snowmobile or tracked vehicles; back then, CB radio operators helped coordinate food runs and assistance to country dwellers stranded in their homes.

In March 1993, the "Storm of the Century" hit Upstate New York. This huge weather event was forecast for days in advance and involved the entire East Coast. However, in Wayne County, lake-effect snow gave it a distinct boost. My notes from that time recall the strangely oppressive stillness before the storm as I walked outside a few hours before it struck. The blizzard began in the afternoon, and by nightfall, the wind was bellowing through the trees and driving clouds of powder across the land. The wind shrieked and roared around my ridgetop house, and drafts from the storm reached completely across the living room from north-facing windows. Several times, I felt the house tremble as a gust slammed against it, and twice I saw a flash of winter lightning made a sickly greenish color by the heavy snow.

The next morning, a drift behind my garage reached nearly to the roof line, and several small patches of snow driven under the door by the blow stretched halfway across the garage floor. After the wind dropped, I sallied forth with my shovel to attack my driveway and spent several hours shoveling densely packed snow off my roof.

Although Buffalo gets all the publicity, Syracuse actually receives more lake-effect snow each winter. Averages here run about 125 inches a season. Usually, sometime around the end of January or early February, Lake Erie freezes over with ice, cutting off the evaporation needed to create snow. Lake Ontario, however, with depths up to eight hundred feet, has a much greater volume of water and usually retains enough warmth to prevent ice formation over much of its surface. This keeps the snow-making machinery going all winter for Oswego and Syracuse to enjoy.

In 2015, a persistent Arctic "vortex" produced a very cold winter, and ice covered 90 percent of the lake. The field of white floes stretched to the horizon, and masses of ice piled up along the shore to form caves and "volcanoes" and small frozen mountains. Every year, people find this new "land" irresistible and venture forth to explore it. This is a stupid thing to do. The ice slabs along the shore that may be ten feet thick sometimes join together with sizable gaps between them that are covered with a thin crust of snow. The unwary, lone ice walker can easily break through, fall in and be trapped between the masses of ice. So don't yield to temptation. Stay on shore and admire it from afar.

Another excellent reason for staying off the seemingly solid open lake ice is the possibility of a wind shift moving it all offshore. Every year, it seems, stories like the following make the paper somewhere on the Great Lakes. This incident occurred on Lake Erie in 2009.

> *A miles-wide ice floe broke away Saturday from Lake Erie's shoreline, trapping more than 130 fishermen offshore, some for as long as four hours. One man fell into the water and later died of an apparent heart attack. A Coast Guard spokesman, Chief Petty Officer Robert Lanier, said 134 people had been plucked from the ice by late afternoon. Rescuers in helicopters lowered baskets onto the ice, and people climbed in and were lifted to safety. Others boarded air boats that glided across the ice.*

"We were in no danger," said one of the rescued anglers. "We knew there was enough ice out there."

His comments notwithstanding, anyone hiking alone is very much in danger no matter how much ice is out there. The ice only has to move a few yards to change your world—and your life expectancy. Your author and her spouse once went rambling around on a thick cover of lake ice. Viewed from a lofty bluff, we saw white solid ice stretched unbroken to the horizon more than ten miles away. However, once on it, we discovered the footing was terrible. A lumpy surface of glazed globs of rock-hard water made a perfect ankle-turning environment. We soon headed back to shore. The next day, every bit of ice had vanished, blown offshore by a south wind.

This lake ice-pressure ridge in March 2015 formed as an ice field shifted and began to melt at winter's end. *Photo by Susan P. Gateley.*

The best way to enjoy ice sculptures is from the shore. *Photo by Susan P. Gateley.*

Ice cover or lack of the same has ecological effects on Lake Ontario beyond simply contributing to the amount of snow on your driveway. The floating ice that blows ashore to form thick "anchor ice" creates a natural breakwater to protect shorelines from erosion during the season of heaviest storm-wave action. Less ice means more erosion for natural shorelines and more sedimentation transport into channels and bays. Some species of fish—the whitefish and the small, herring-like cisco—depend on ice cover for successful reproduction. And animals move over ice to and from islands in the lake in search of new homes and habitats. A few years ago, during our annual June visits, I noticed that many turtle nests on Main Duck Island had been dug up by some predator. A fellow cruiser informed us that a fox had made his way to the island the year before and was apparently hitting the reptile egg supply pretty hard.

Ice scour scrapes off hordes of pesky plankton-eating zebra mussels from the nearshore shallows and reduces their numbers. (See chapter 11 for more on their harmful impacts on the lake's native fishes.) People use ice, too, for fishing and for sports like ice boating and snowmobiling. However, even in protected bays, thin ice causes accidents and some deaths every season.

Seasonal levels of the lake approach their lowest point around December. Beaches then are wide and empty of human users, inviting the solitary beachcomber to stroll by still waters on a calm day. Flocks of long-tailed ducks, scaup and the odd herring gull, nature's own ice sculptures and perhaps a bit of wreckage cast up by storm waves, add interest to the winter lake and beach. And come late February or March, shore ice and shadows begin to retreat, perhaps the first cries of returning ringbill gulls sound overhead and the annual cycle continues.

6

THE RESTLESS BEACH

Lake Ontario is defined by more than seven hundred miles of shoreline. Its northeastern coast features outcrops of limestone like that of the Canadian shore east of the Bay of Quinte. These rocky ledges and cliffs often front directly on the water, leaving little in the way of beaches. But much of the New York shoreline has extensive stretches of gravel and sand beach, some of which are accessible to the public at a dozen parks and wildlife management areas.

No land form in our region is more ephemeral and subject to change than these beaches. Much of the fascination with our lake's coast is its endless shape-shifting, as sand, silt, pebbles and boulders are moved around by wind and water. Stretches of sand prevail on the south shore at Hamlin Beach State Park, near the Genesee River, at Sodus Point and at Fair Haven's state park. The sandy hills of Irondequoit and Webster and the beach at Charlotte owe their existence to the sediment load of the Genesee River that, during the Ice Age, entered the lake through a valley now occupied by Irondequoit Creek. At the lake's east end, miles of sand beach mostly derived from south-shore bluffs have accumulated and persisted.

At some locations like Sodus Point, man-made structures and changes to the shore might be causing sand to accumulate. However, at least three locations on the lake—its east end, the western side of Prince Edward County and the Toronto Islands/archipelago—seem to have had sandy shores long before any human modification of the coasts occurred. In

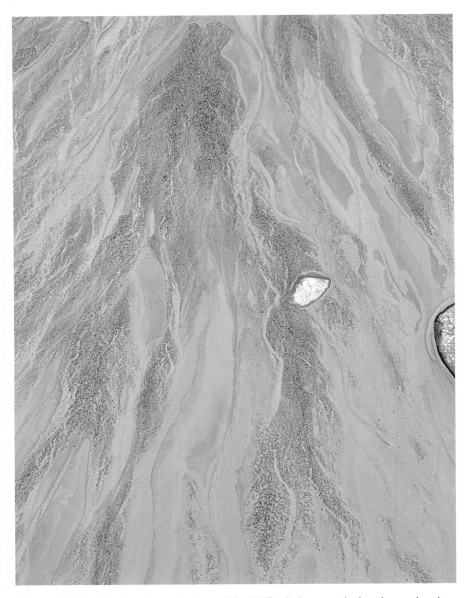

The small "deltas" and washes at the foot of the bluff exist because the heavier sand grains trace the path of the flowing water's miniature channels through the finer clay particles. *Photo by Susan P. Gateley.*

these areas, currents and longshore drift have worked to transport and deposit sand after its erosion.

While the beach itself may change, individual grains of sand are all but indestructible. Lake Ontario beach sand is mineral sand. If you take a hand lens and peer at a pinch of it, you'll see a variety of sand grain colors, each color representing a mineral. Our sand is made up of reddish garnet, dark hornblende, light-colored quartz and other minerals. Each grain was created by the breakdown and weathering of ancient rocks.

The sand, gravel and cobbles of the lake's south shore erode mainly from the adjacent shoreline, though some also comes from the lake bottom near shore. Moved and mixed by the glacier, this "till" was originally deposited during the ice's retreat. If you look closely at a mud flow at the foot of a lakeshore bluff after a heavy rain, you'll see sorting in action. The mud flow often looks a lot like an outwash area below a desert highlands as seen from thirty thousand feet during a transcontinental flight. The flow patterns are caused by the same mechanisms of sorting.

Once sand makes it to the beach, it's subject to the forces of both water and wind. If there's enough beach sand to dry out, it then readily moves inland with the wind to form dunes. Sometimes, you may notice small, darker patches on the surface of the beach. I once thought this was some form of pollution, perhaps oil or tar, deposited on the sand. But these purplish or black smudge marks are more likely to be the result of mineral sorting. Sand grains of garnet or other dark minerals that are heavier than lighter-colored minerals are sorted by density when subject to gentle swashing of wavelets. The result can be small patches of darker sand.

The experts tell us that our sand is far more ancient than many of the beach pebbles underfoot. Derived from mountain rocks and inland outcrops, shifted and shoved by running water and then, just a moment ago in geologic time, released from a shoreline bluff, the sand now moves on along the shore propelled by longshore transport currents. Lake Ontario sand is "sharp" sand. It's been waterborne during its long life. Windblown sand grains like those of the desert or some marine beaches are more rounded. Such sand makes an inferior mortar mix and so is less valuable to commerce. Concrete is a mixture of powdered limestone cement and sand, and "sharp" sand makes far more durable mortar.

During a recent spell of gentrification in the twenty-first century, a neighborhood in San Diego called North Park saw many of the little craftsman bungalows that dated to the early 1900 jacked up and given new

Sand grain sorting from water action collects denser mineral grains to form the dark smudge seen at lower left. *Photo by Susan P. Gateley.*

foundations. Their original concrete footers had cracked and crumbled over the years, because they were made of local wind-rounded sea beach sand.

As you stand on the lake's eastern sandy shores or slog through the loose sand of Prince Edward County's big dunes, it's hard to imagine that there is a shortage of sand. However, experts tell us that, next to water, it is now the most widely used natural resource in the world. Relentless construction booms have led to sand wars and shortages in India, Indonesia, China and elsewhere. Construction firms have dug up beaches, dredged rivers and pushed into agricultural areas to strip-mine sand deposits. Sometimes, farmers and other landowners who objected have ended up mysteriously murdered. Some have claimed that by the end of the twenty-first century the natural beach will have become extinct from sand mining and other causes. Fortunately, we in New York State still seem to have plenty of sand suitable for mortar mixes, though other man-made forces do threaten Lake Ontario's sand beaches.

Watch the sand on a windy day. You'll see it moving, flowing, eddying, sometimes rising several feet off the ground, as individual grains glitter in the sun. Park your car near the beach on such a day and you may hear the constant hiss of sand grains striking your door. And just try to walk against the wind over the dry sand when it's blowing hard. The sting of sand against your face is brutal. Beaches everywhere are shifty places, like the water itself. The lake's shoreline is constantly changing through erosion and accretion. During a single storm, the lake can shift tons of gravel sediment and bury your favorite sand patch under a pile of large, rounded cobbles in a few hours.

Most of the lake's south shore from Oswego to the west is made of gravel and cobble. One very obvious change you can see if you visit the same stretch of gravel beach is the formation and disappearance of berms. These short-lived ridges of gravel run parallel to the shore. Often, portions of the berm are made up of pebbles of strikingly uniform size that have been sorted by wave energy. The berm represents the upper reach of the surf generated by the most recent storm. Sometimes on a wide beach you may see two or three such berms of varying heights, each representing a recent storm event. If a berm consists of those bigger, hard-to-walk-on cobbles, you know a major gale pounded that shore recently.

As you observe the berms, you'll see that the larger stones are often located near the top of the ridge. This is because when the big waves first strike, they have more energy to push those heavier rocks inland. As the water withdraws and flows back into the lake, it drags and sorts the smaller, lighter pebbles and deposits them low on the shore near the water's edge.

Pebble sorting at Port Bay. *Photo by Susan P. Gateley.*

A snapper working on the excavation of a nest on a pebble beach. *Photo by Susan P. Gateley*.

In a really heavy surf, the waves may even wash entirely over a barrier bar on the lake, pushing the bigger stones over the top of the berm and down into the marsh. Berm formation is influenced by wave intensity and wind direction, lake-water levels, seiches and neighboring landforms. They rarely persist for long before the pebbles are mixed up and moved on again by another storm.

Pebble beaches are not friendly to life, as the small stones are constantly on the move, grinding and crushing as they go. Most creatures that visit the beach use it briefly as a meeting place or a spot to sunbathe. Water snakes, geese, turtles or herons may pause here to fish, seek a mate or simply hang out. Turtles may also visit in the spring to use the higher, more stable parts of the beach to lay eggs, and foxes forage for dead fish, birds and fresh turtle eggs. But, like humans, they soon move on to more stable environments.

HUMAN IMPACTS ON THE BEACH

The restless movement of freshly eroded sediment renews the natural beach constantly. Beachcombers can come back to the same spot to find a new crop of fossils, pretty pebbles and cast-up bits of man-made junk week after week. It's all part of the magic and mystery of that ephemeral edge between land and water. But when people build houses near the water and pay hefty property tax bills for their view of the lake, they expect their land to stay put. Inevitably, after their private beach shows nomadic tendencies, owners become alarmed and indignant, especially after the lake gnaws away at the waterfront property line. After a few years, the winter waves creep closer to the cottage or McMansion. The ultimate result, depending on the homeowner's finances and political clout, is either retreat and abandonment or a seawall or boulders to stabilize the shoreline.

Since the last Ice Age, lakeshore erosion has been a constant, especially along the Canadian shore west of the Bay of Quinte and on the east and south shores that are made up of glacial till. This mix of dirt and rock, much to the chagrin of lakefront landowners, erodes readily, sometimes at the rate of two feet or more per year. The eroded material is carried away by the lake to form more of those restless gravel and sand beaches.

Because people insist on building various "permanent" structures like roads, sewer lines and houses on coasts subject to erosion, a whole scientific discipline has arisen devoted to the study of beaches. Geomorphology uses physics and lots of math to understand and create models of how erosion works. The engineers and scientists also use the term *sediment budget* to describe the ways in which gravel and sand wander along the shore. Interest in sand budgets arose because of some very costly engineering failures on saltwater coasts over the last hundred years or so.

Lake Ontario beaches move because of a current that runs along the shoreline on windy days. The current is created when waves formed by westerly winds come in from the open lake at an angle to the land. When the waves strike along the lake's straight south coast, they generate a west-to-east flow that carries sand and gravel with it. The movement of sediment is called longshore drift. As waves hit at an angle, they move sediment into coves behind points, and wave energy is concentrated on points, causing them to erode more rapidly. The result is that the entire shoreline's features remain constant relative to the rest of the shore.

At its most basic, a sand or sediment budget consists of inputs of sediment from erosion and losses of sand that are carried by the longshore drift current

The barrier bar at Sodus Bay looking west. It was recently breached east of the channel during record high water. *Photo by Susan P. Gateley.*

into either deep water or the protected water of a bay or harbor, where it's no longer subject to longshore transport. Studies have shown that much of the sediment moved along the south shore of the lake comes from the bluffs and drumlin ends that front the shore, with the rest coming from bottom scour. Very little comes from rivers here.

Historically, the sediment budget stayed pretty "balanced," as bluffs eroded continuously to build beaches and barrier bars. But since the onset of waterfront development, especially since the 1950s, the overall supply of sediment available for beach building has been reduced. In some areas, shoreline erosion has increased and protective natural barrier bars have gone missing.

After European settlement, people built dozens of harbors with more or less permanent channels protected by piers or jetties around the lake. When sediment carried along by the longshore current encountered one of these harbors and its jetties, some of the material piled up behind the jetty. And some, especially the lighter sand and silt, found its way around the end of the jetty and entered the channel and harbor. Once the sand got into the harbor, it was lost to the system, while the material trapped behind the jetty was also no longer available for beach building "downstream." At the entrances to

Sodus Bay channel, showing sediment accretion on the west side. The original "natural" barrier bar is visible to the south of the man-made channel. *Photo by Susan P. Gateley.*

both Sodus and Little Sodus Bay, one can clearly see the buildup of sandy drift as it's been pushed by prevailing west winds up against the western channel jetties. At the same time, the historic gravel and sand barrier bar to the east of the channel has vanished and been replaced by a cement seawall.

When the sediment supply is reduced, beaches grow smaller and may vanish altogether. Engineers call the beach itself a "protective feature," with good reason. Waves strike the gradual slope and expend much or all of their energy before striking the land. Without the beach, the waves slam directly against the land, speeding erosion.

In a natural system, most of the erosion of the lakeshore is caused by runoff that carries sand, clay and gravel down from the top of the bank or bluff to the beach. A great deal of this action occurs in the spring, especially as the frozen bluff face begins to thaw. After it hits the beach, this material is then carried off by the longshore current. However, in the last few decades, homeowners and some municipal entities have built seawalls and placed boulders along their shorelines to prevent further erosion and shoreline recession. In the effort to control their beach, they destroy it. Unfortunately, they destroy their neighbors' beaches, too. This in turn accelerates the erosion of those neighboring shorelines.

Recently, the federal government spent over $9 million to restore the barrier beach of Braddock's Bay. Studies showed that the protective bar here vanished around 1900 after harbor channels and hardening of shorelines reduced the amount of sediment available. After the marshes behind a bar lose their beaches and are open to the waves of the lake, their emergent vegetation is torn away and their sediments stirred up, creating degraded, turbid, silty shallows. Silt smothers some of the marsh bottom life that is essential to the nursery areas used by many of the lake's fishes. Muddy, turbid water also prevents light from reaching the bottom to support rooted vegetation vital to the nearshore food chain, even as it prevents sight-feeding fish and birds like the osprey and eagle from finding their fish dinners.

The wave-swept, degraded marsh ecosystem of Braddock's Bay was simplified and destabilized by the loss of vegetation and clear water. Amphibians, waterfowl, fur bearers like the mink and muskrats and many other marsh residents could no longer thrive in this environment. The open embayment also had become a sand "sink," as sediments swept into it dropped out of the system and were no longer available for beach building on adjacent lands. And the waterfront property owners on the bay were

Fresh slumps are visible on this bluff undercut by wave action after it lost its protective beach. *Photo by Susan P. Gateley.*

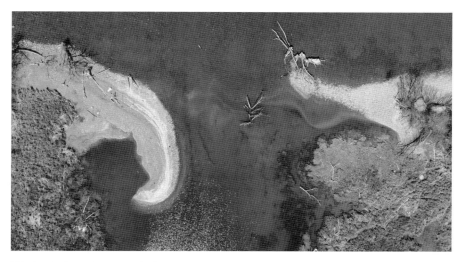

The hook-shaped gravel spit (*left*) shows sediment moving into a marsh formerly blocked by a protective bar, as indicated by the two dead willow remains. *Photo by Chris Gateley*.

subject to accelerated erosion once it opened to the lake. The taxpayers weren't happy. Eventually, other taxpayers came up with federal money from the Great Lakes Restoration Initiative to "restore" their barrier bar.

Construction began in 2016 of a nearly 1,700-foot artificial barrier bar created out of rubble to close off Braddock's Bay. A gap allowed boating access to the protected shallows of the bay. Since then, planting of various native marsh plants and control of invasives has been undertaken. In just a few years, monitoring has shown an increase in variety and abundances of amphibian and bird species using the newly protected marsh areas.

WONDROUS WILLOWS

On natural, undeveloped barrier bars and along shorelines, willows help hold the land together. The willow is one of the toughest trees on the planet. Arctic willows that grow six inches high can live for over two hundred years. In my childhood, I climbed the low branches of a large willow tree that grew by a creek in our backyard. Its trunk was certainly four feet in diameter. Then, one day, after a severe ice storm, it split to the ground, forming two halves in the 1960s. It was still growing forty years later. It could easily be a century old, since I remember it being huge over fifty years ago.

Most of our beach willows are probably hybrids. Willows often hybridize. Our native black willow tree doesn't get real big and lacks the silvery leaf underside that the willows growing on the lake's barrier bars display. These large beach willows may be hybrids, perhaps originating from native trees and European species like the white willow, which does have leaves with a silvery underside. Whatever their ancestry, these willows, along with the occasional cottonwood, are the only trees I've seen commonly growing on the natural barrier bars of the lake. (I define "natural" as a shifting, eroding, "living" bar, the normal condition on the lake before the era of human intervention in the form of shoreline stabilization.)

Though its lumber is scoffed at by firewood users and by most fine woodworking artisans, willow has been used by humans for millennia. Baskets, fish weirs, nets and artists' charcoal have been made from willow. I've seen very credible fabric-covered canoes and kayaks made of willow withies, no doubt inspired by the ancient "bowl boats," known as coracles, that date to the Bronze Age. In Denmark, I saw garden privacy fences woven from coppiced willow stems. And nowhere have I seen a tree take more punishment than willows do on the shores of Lake Ontario.

Because of constant erosion from wave action, the south shore of the lake between Sodus Bay and Fair Haven historically has receded at one to two feet a year. The gravel and cobble barrier bars that form across the mouths of creeks and marshes go with it. As do the willows. About twenty years ago, I paddled along the shore one spring and observed that every willow along the barrier bar of Red Creek Marsh had tipped over. A whole row of root bases was lined up here, as nearly every tree fell inwards away from the lake. Heavy surf from a big storm had washed away the gravel around their roots, causing the trees to fall over. Some of the bar's gravel had been flung over the top of the bar and into the marsh. (Engineers call this "overwash.") Some countless tons of more sediment had been moved away to the east by the waves through sediment transport. But the willows lying supine with their roots in the air and the sunshine did not die. Instead, they began to root once more, putting sprouts out along their now-buried stems and branches. (Willows and cottonwoods are among the few trees that can fix nitrogen from the air, allowing them to thrive on our nutrient-poor gravel beaches.)

Two decades later, willows again grew on the bar. Some trees had sprouted up straight and tall, thirty feet high and six inches in diameter, from the

This March 2020 photo shows new woody growth on willows that fell inward and were buried by gravel about fifteen years ago. *Photo by Susan P. Gateley.*

buried trunks. And they were ready to move again, as possibly they have done for hundreds of years.

It's little wonder that the willow has such a large body of folklore and myth associated with it. In Japan and China, numerous stories exist of willows as a source of life and wisdom. In English folklore, some willows are believed to be sinister entities capable of uprooting themselves and stalking travelers. At least here by Lake Ontario, they do seem able to undertake travels of a sort. Here, walking willow trees help hold the barrier bars together to protect the biodiversity of the marshes behind them. This benefits various insects, birds and animals that feed on the trees. Beavers strip the bark from their shoots, while muskrats nibble on their twigs. The beautiful, big, green cecropia moth caterpillars munch on their leaves, and birds pick insects from their leaves or pause to rest among their branches. The kingfisher often perches on a shore-side tree in search of a fish dinner.

On a small marsh fed by a little creek that empties into the lake near Wolcott, the barrier bar vanished in the winter of 2018–19. It is likely that the cause of the missing bar lies upstream, where a substantial amount of

A willow log deposited on the beach during the winter showing sprouts of new growth by August. *Photo by Susan P. Gateley.*

shoreline hardening by waterfront homeowners and across Port Bay has taken place recently, reducing the supply of eroded gravel. The missing bar now lies under a couple feet of water. Before it vanished, a large old willow had established itself at about the midpoint of the bar. Its trunk was easily three feet in diameter. For perhaps a century it had steadily retreated with the bar, moving south perhaps two hundred feet over the years. When the bar abruptly vanished in the late fall of 2018, the willow was left standing in two to three feet of water. Soon, the winter waves began battering it. A smaller neighboring willow split and disintegrated. The old willow also split but clung tenaciously to the submerged gravel. Surf from fall gales crashed into it. Then ice formed along the shore and briefly protected it from the worst winter storms. In the early spring, the constant hammering began again. I saw massive globs of ice frozen from spray flung high into its few remaining limbs. I saw three-foot waves smash against it for days on end. And on a quiet day in June when I visited the still-open creek, I saw green leaves on its few tortured, broken limbs remaining above the water.

It lived all summer, its roots completely submerged by the lake. Another winter came. This time, only a brief period of ice formation occurred along the shore. This time, the willow had to endure an even crueler beating. In March, when I wrote this, a couple of battered branches were still visible above the water. I wondered if they would leaf out again. Amazingly, they did.

These are some of the toughest, hardiest trees on the planet. Perhaps they can serve as an example of how we, too, can endure the difficult days of our lives.

7

STONY SHORES

Our freshwater beaches lack the varied life of the ocean's coasts. No welks or wavy turbans, no sand dollars or skate egg cases are cast ashore by the waves here. Only a few small, bleached zebra and quagga mussel shells or the rare freshwater clam tempt the beach walker here. Sometimes, though, in spring or late summer, a few small flocks of far-flying shorebirds flit along the water's edge as they do on saltwater. They stop only briefly during their migrations by the lake.

Our pebble beaches of the south shore are too shifty and unstable to foster much in the way of permanent residents. But where the beach separates the lake from a protected marsh or swamp, a few creatures use the beach to meet and greet with others of their kind. On such barrier bar beaches you may encounter lounging Canada geese families or a blue heron standing statue-still at the water's edge as it awaits a passing minnow. One day in June some years ago, I encountered a group of northern water snakes having a beach party. (Our native water snakes are harmless and, in my experience at least, very shy, unlike the venomous water moccasin of more southerly waters.) On this bright afternoon, the warming water and hot sun on the pebbles had heated their own passions. Snake sex was very much in evidence. The smaller snakes, presumably cuing in on a chemical trace, were eagerly following the trails of larger females. While I watched, several small groups of reptiles engaged in sensuous couplings and twining around each other even as at least a dozen loners crept around searching for a partner of their own. It was positively titillating to observe the snakes celebrating the longest days of early summer. Clearly, it was high time to make more snakes.

A few days later when I visited the beach, all was still, and the party was long gone. The only trace of the momentous gang bang was a few vertebrae and bits of drying snake meat. Perhaps a late partygoer stayed too long and was spotted by one of the resident eagles who were also frequent visitors to this particular beach.

Another reptile that makes some use of the beach for reproduction is the turtle. I've seen nesting turtles using beaches on Little Sodus Bay and in Canada, but only well above the reach of high water. The inner faces of the gravel south-shore beaches adjacent to a swale or marsh might also provide nesting sites.

One small resident of the south-shore pebble beaches you can count on seeing each summer is the wolf spider. But you have to look sharp, as these little creatures flicker out of sight among the stones at lightning speed. As a child, I tried in vain to capture one so as to get a good look at it. Later, I grew patient enough to sit quietly for a few minutes. Then the little hunters would creep out from under their rocks to bask in the sun. They do most of their foraging at night, and if you walk a woodland driveway with an

A mother wolf spider with baby spiderlets on her back. *Photo by Susan P. Gateley.*

LED headlight, their eyes reflect the light as tiny bright spots among the leaf litter and weeds. The beach spiders are not very big, maybe an inch or so in diameter, and I've never known anyone to experience a spider bite while sitting among them. (The internet says their bite can be painful, so I wouldn't try very hard to catch one.)

The wolf spider doesn't spin a web. As its name suggests, it runs down its insect prey, and if you watch them on the beach ducking for cover, you can see that they are fast movers. One article I read describes them as "athletic," which seems apt. This group of arachnids is common in woodlands, lawns and gardens. Many species are territorial. Last summer, I encountered a wolf spider regularly among my garden beets. While weeding the vegetables, I've often seen the female spiders carrying their round, white egg sacs to safety. After the young break out of the egg sac, they climb on to their mother's back and remain with her for several weeks or months, depending on the species. Then one day, when the right summer or early fall day comes along with blue skies and gentle winds, the baby spiders abandon their mother's back and disperse in search of grass or weed stems to climb. After they reach the top, they spin a long thread of silk and are then borne off by the wind to their various destinies. The beach spiders can live for more than one season, and I've seen half-sized ones out and about on the beach in March. The unfortunate males often don't survive after mating and frequently end up as dinner for the female.

Stone Stories

The lake's south-shore beaches with their colorful variety of rocks are a pebble picker's delight. As it moved southwest, the glacier picked up rocks from different locations. When it melted away, the rocks remained behind, dumped together in a multicultural mix. Ancient metamorphic gneiss (rhymes with "mice") from the Thousand Islands area and the Canadian shield, granite and dark sparkly schist from the Adirondacks and Ordovician limestone from the Canadian side of the lake now lie side by side on the beach. They and other sedimentary and metamorphic rocks create a delightful mosaic of colors, textures and shapes on south-shore beaches.

Around Sackets Harbor and Chaumont as well as on the Canadian shore around Kingston and eastern Prince Edward County, gray limestone pebbles predominate. Most of the beach pebbles on New York's south shore are of either various colors of sedimentary sandstone or limestone or have metamorphic origins. Sometimes, the keen-eyed beachcomber may also see a few rocks of human origins. You might occasionally encounter water-rounded bits of concrete or brick that recall the fate of a cottage or some other man-made structure that once stood on an eroding shore. I've found odd water-rounded "pumice"-like clinkers and bits of slag as well as pieces of gray dolomite rock broken off of some of the boulders that have been imported by people to protect shorelines. Once or twice, I've found water-rounded gray beach stones from these imported boulders that have hollows, or "vugs," containing small crystals. So you never know what oddities might show up among the native sandstone or other pebbles left by the glacier on the neighborhood beach.

Freshly eroded rocks recently released from the shoreline banks and bluffs usually have angular shapes and edges. After a few years of beach life, they become the water-rounded pebbles that skitter and roll so readily underfoot. However, a close look at the stones still embedded in the bluff's clay reveal that some of them show signs of some water-rounding that must have occurred long before Lake Ontario existed. Now and then, a really big rock ends up on the shore or in the lake. They can be of various types; some are sandstone or limestone, others are metamorphic granite or gneiss. These are glacial erratics, some of which were carried long distances by the ice.

Not long ago, I encountered two refrigerator-sized boulders recently eroded out from the shoreline. Both appeared to be of identical granite-like rock, ancient metamorphic rocks that may have originated from the Canadian Shield to the north. Both were clearly somewhat water- or ice-rounded.

I thought they looked like siblings. Perhaps they were both broken off of a larger mass of rock eons ago by the glacier. Perhaps they were then dragged around and shaped by the ice. Or perhaps, after forming a billion year ago miles below the earth's surface in the deep time of geology, they somehow journeyed to the surface to then be shaped by water action. Maybe at some point in their lives they were subjected to the forces of an ancient river's current or were once pounded by the surf of an unknown ocean. Perhaps they were rounded off by the warm waves of the sunlit Ordovician Sea, where the fossil crinoids and horn corals of today once lived. At any rate, for at least the last hundred centuries or so, they made their journey through time as a couple. As the New York State Museum guide to New York fossils says, "The vastness of geologic time is difficult to comprehend."

These two distinctly rounded glacial erratics of metamorphic rock have recently been washed out from the land. *Photo by Susan P. Gateley.*

The origins and types of glacial erratics differ from the so-called native bedrock. Before the age of geological science, people thought these odd boulders were deposited by the great flood that Noah navigated. By the later 1800s, scholars figured out that they had been transported by ice, sometimes for hundreds of miles, before being left behind after the big meltdown. While such rocks can be the size of a house, most of the ones along the lakeshore are more on the order of a compact car or smaller. There is a particularly big one just offshore from Dutch Street that lies in about seven feet of water. It's visible during fall water levels and is far enough out to be a year-round navigational hazard to small boats. The ones in my photo are much more typical. The erratics were eroded or plucked from the earth by the moving ice sheet after perhaps its massive weight cracked the rock below it.

Among the most common rocks on the south-shore beaches are those of greenish-gray Oswego sandstone or pinkish-brown Medina-type sandstone. Most of the best skipping stones are either sandstone or limestone, since

These glacial erratics were deposited directly atop limestone ledges in Canada. *Photo by Susan P. Gateley.*

sedimentary rocks typically form layered deposits and so are more likely to split into thin pieces than are the older crystalline metamorphic pebbles. Another somewhat harder sedimentary rock often encountered on these shores is from the Potsdam sandstone formation, carried to the south shore from the St. Lawrence River Valley in northern New York. It's often banded with off-white and pale orange or pink colors. One way to identify a sandstone pebble is to rub the surface to feel for the slight grit of the individual sand grains. After sandstone is metamorphosed, it becomes hard-polished quartzite, which also comes in various colors.

Some of the abundant reddish-brown sandstones may contain "trace" fossils—holes or irregularities left by burrowing worms or insects that tunneled through the sand millions of years ago. Larger sandstone rocks recently eroded from the bluffs may also show fossilized dried mud cracks or rippled surfaces originally formed by wind or water flowing over the sand. Of course, once such a rock makes it to the beach, wave action will make short work of such surface textures.

The other common sedimentary pebbles encountered on New York's beaches are those of gray or black limestone. Our region lies atop several layers of limestone dating back three to four hundred million years. On

Sandstone pebbles, including a banded pebble from the St. Lawrence Valley area to the north (*upper left*). *Photo by Susan P. Gateley.*

A Canadian cement quarry on the Bay of Quinte. *Photo by Susan P. Gateley.*

the lake's Canadian shore, where a thick limestone layer lies at the surface, several large waterfront quarries and plants produce cement from these rocks that is then shipped to various ports on the lake, including Oswego and Rochester, as powdered cargo via freighters and barges.

Limestone is made up of the calcareous remains of marine creatures. Once during the Ordovician era, vast numbers of corals, crinoids, clam-like bivalves, snail-like gastropods and other creatures with shells thrived here in a shallow sunlit sea. After they died, their remains were pulverized into powder and eventually compacted into rock. Some of the gray limestone pebbles on the lake's beaches contain traces of these creatures.

Each rock layer has its own distinctive association of fossils, and geologists have used fossils to date rock layers. The fossils were formed when silt or sediment buried them millions of years ago. There are two types of common fossils on Lake Ontario's shores. As the organisms decayed, a "cast" or a mold sometimes formed around their remains, creating an imprint in the rock surface. Or their substance was actually replaced by minerals like whitish crystalline calcite, leaving a fossil embedded in the rock. Under certain conditions, pyrite (fool's gold) replaces some of the tissues. I've seen one or two large cephalopod fossils containing a glint of pyrite. The shiny pyrite (iron sulfide) readily oxidizes when exposed to air, however, and soon turns into a dull rust-colored iron sulfate.

Sometimes, the lighter-colored fossils in gray limestone are indistinct and hard to make out against the rock matrix. They may be mashed up into a "fossil hash," or you may find a rock filled with small fragments of the original organisms. Still, if you study the rock closely, you may pick out a distinctive round disc that once was part of a segmented sea-lily stem or some other fragment of a once-living creature.

The sea lily (crinoid), a relative of the starfish, once flourished in vast abundances in the ancient seas. The various crinoid species were somewhat mop-like when living. Most were attached to the seabed and had a long stem made up of cylindrical segments and a "head" of feathery arms used to filter food from the water. Sea lilies and mobile "feather stars" still live in various marine habitats today, but not in the numbers of their Ordovician ancestors.

Another fairly common fossil is that of the flattened coil shape of a gastropod shell. An inch or two in diameter, it can stand out clearly like a miniature petrified galaxy spiral in stone. Many of the common beach pebble fossils are quite small, but now and then a cephalopod fossil six inches or more may catch your eye. These animals were distant ancestors of the present-day squid-like nautilus. Most of the fossil cephalopods found on the

A limestone pebble with cross sections of crinoid stems. Their tissues have been replaced by calcite. *Photo by Susan P. Gateley.*

south shore had straight, tapered, cone-like shells, but you may find a few larger coiled shells that resemble the chambered nautilus. Both these and the horn-like straight shells contain chambers formed as the animal grew that are often very distinctive.

Beachcombers also may find soft, brown, chalky rocks that contain many small fossil shell molds and imprints. As described earlier, sandstone "trace" fossils are also present on our beaches. They're best seen in rocks recently eroded from the shore.

Lake Ontario's legendary lucky stones, black pebbles circled by a complete white ring, are mostly darker limestone. The white ring is made up of calcite crystals and formed after the rock was cracked underground. Over time, mineralized water left deposits of calcite in the joint that then hardened in a process not unlike the formation of stalactites or soda straws in a cave. The calcite glued the two parts of the rock back together to create a "healed" rock. Our lucky stone beach pebbles were fortunate to be knitted back together after being broken by extreme stress in the distant past. Some of the bigger boulders along the shore also show mineral veins of contrasting colors. Quartz and calcite are two common light-colored minerals found in beach rock veins.

A photo of a dolomite boulder with is a "cast," or mold-type fossil. *Photo by Susan P. Gateley*.

Selection of Lake Ontario lucky rocks. *Photo by Susan P. Gateley*.

Beachcombers along the lake's south shore can also see a wide variety of colorful metamorphic rocks. Some sparkle with crystals of feldspar or mica. Some contain gleaming bits of pyrite. Pink, purple, white, black, even pale-green pebbles delight sharp-eyed stone seekers. Schist beach pebbles are "foliate" (layered) and often darkly colored by mineral hornblende. They were carried by the glacier from the Adirondacks. They often contain pockets of tiny reddish garnet crystals. Other mineral crystals embedded in schist pebbles, including mica, often catch the eye with their silvery glitters and sparkles.

Gneiss pebbles transported from the Canadian Shield area or the Thousand Islands region are among the oldest surface rocks in North America. Billion-plus-year-old gneiss pebbles often look like granite, depending on how intensely the rock was melted and metamorphosed during its long life. It, too, is a foliated rock often tinted with orange or pink and marked with black streaks.

Among my memorable finds while pebble picking have been several water-rounded quartz crystals that looked exactly like the Delaware Bay "diamonds" hawked in Cape May souvenir shops. They had a frosted look that made me think at first I had found a piece of "water glass." Perhaps they

Many Wayne and Monroe County cobblestone houses often have façades made of lake-rounded beach cobbles. *Photo by Susan P. Gateley.*

originated from vugs embedded within some of the gray dolomite boulders brought in from nearby quarries in increasing quantities to harden the lake's shore. Not long ago, a friend of mine picked up a distinctly green pebble that looked like pale jade. Was it serpentine, we wondered? According to the internet, a dike of igneous rock runs north from the Syracuse area up into the Adirondacks. Perhaps our "jade" came from the North Country with the glacier and ended up inside a drumlin.

One of the oddest beach pebbles I ever saw was a rounded, brown sandstone cobble about the size and shape of a goose egg. It contained a small hole that in turn contained a tiny, water-rounded pebble. No matter how we turned and rattled and shook it, we could not extract the little stone. A water-rounded rock within a rock was just a bit too weird for me.

A number of websites and forums offer information if you wish to learn more about our local fossils and rocks. One that I found useful is the New York section of The Fossil Forum, online at http://www.thefossilforum.com.

8

LAKESHORE WETLANDS

On each side of the narrow barrier bars of the lake's beaches lie two very different worlds. Inland the sheltered waters of swamps, streams and marshes are cut off from the lake and protected from it. Offshore, in sharp contrast, lies the wide, windswept, open lake whose cold waters are relatively barren. Turn about to examine the marsh a few feet away and you see that life abounds. Darting dragonflies glitter and flash in the sun, marsh wrens chatter and bullfrogs boast of their greatness. If you dip a small bucket of water and examine it with a ten-power hand lens, you'll see an astonishing abundance of animal life. These detritus-laden waters are a living soup. Dozens of tiny organisms wriggle, crawl, dart and thrash around in your pail. Pinhead-sized ostracods looking like tiny clams trundle along the bottom of the container. Cladocerans dash around their miniature sea, while copepods dart in jerky spurts through the depths. Your container's contents are a constant swirl of life. Add a handful of water weeds, and a half-dozen varieties of tiny insect larvae, small damselflies, larger dragonflies, midges and a school of shrimp-like scuds come with it to swim among the swarming microcrustraceans. After things settle a bit, the creepy-crawlies appear; planarians, snails, leeches and various worms slip over the bucket bottom. And, of course, there is another world of the invisible. One-celled plants, protozoans, beautiful glass-shelled diatoms, bacteria, fungi and other microscopic creatures thrive within the swamp.

In summer, the marsh becomes a sunlit flower garden of production. Emerald cattail rushes bend to the wind, forming waves and ripples of motion across the prairie-like flats. Among the cattails, swamp loosestrife arches its vines spangled with bright pink flowers. Tall, sturdy, hollyhock-like swamp rose mallow gleams a soft delicate pink against the green. Yellow iris, the lavender-colored flower spikes of pickerel weed and white arrowhead blossoms splash the water's shallows with color. Floating on the edges of open-water channels are the ubiquitous white and yellow water lilies.

The lakeshore marshes are an example of what ecologists call the "edge effect." Wherever two different habitats or ecosystems come together, you often find a richer, more productive area. Here in the marsh, where land and moving water meet, is incredible bounty. Marshes grow more vegetative biomass than the most intensely cultivated farm fields. In one experiment, grasses of a Georgia salt marsh were harvested, dried and weighed. The dry weight of plant material totaled ten tons per acre, far in excess of the one and a half tons of organic material that would be harvested from a cultivated wheat field.

The energy in wetlands comes from gravity's action on running water and from sunlight. Water flowing off surrounding hills, pastures, farm fields and forests transports nutrients to the marsh. And the sun helps power a marvelously efficient and intricate recycling scheme that breaks down debris

White water lilies and small floating plants called duckweed abound in the various lakeshore marshes. *Photo by Susan P. Gateley.*

and dead vegetable matter to make it available to the large, showy flowering plants and the tiny, unseen diatoms of the marsh. The rapid and efficient recycling that takes place here is also what makes marshes so valuable as water purifiers. A marsh acts as a sort of giant filter to cleanse toxins, excessive nutrients, and other impurities from the runoff entering it. Marshes have been called the kidneys of our watersheds. There have even been a number of successful efforts in some areas of the country to use marshes as actual sewage treatment systems.

Marshes also are important in regulating runoff and in the recharge of underground water reservoirs. When a rainstorm sends water cascading down hillsides and rushing off the pavement into a nearby stream, the marsh acts as a sponge to absorb that sudden pulse of runoff. The water is held within its basin to slowly recharge aquifers even as it is purified.

When the lakeshore marsh gets filled up from a heavy rainfall, it sometimes breaches the barrier beach. Water then pours out into the lake in a brief but spectacular rush. I once watched such a breach in progress. Within an hour, the little marshland creek had widened its entrance to the lake from six feet to forty feet across. The force of the fast-draining wetland carried twelve-inch logs off the beach with it, and the outflow was visible for hundreds of feet out into the lake. The water level in the marsh dropped about three feet in a few hours. A week later, winter storms had closed it off again.

In sharp contrast to the lakeshore marsh is another shoreline wetland: the embayed swamp. Like the marsh, it forms when a creek drains into a low area between upland areas. But the volume of water entering the swamp is less than that of the marsh, so it never gets high enough to breach the barrier bar. The level of water changes less quickly than the lakeshore marsh's level as the swamp water seeps and percolates through the gravel into the lake. This more constant water level allows woody shrubs like the buttonwood and alder to gain a foothold in the wetland, shading out the varied diversity of vegetation of the sunlit marsh. Eventually, almost the entire area is filled in, mostly with button bush, some winterberry and perhaps a few alders and red maples.

No other area of the lakeshore seems more mysterious and primeval to me than these odd little swamps. I believe their moss-festooned shrubs have been largely undisturbed since the time of the Cayuga. They may well be the most untouched and least modified of all the habitats existing today along the lakeshore. Though only a few acres in size, the little "swale" might be the truest wilderness left anywhere along the lake's south shore.

Buttonbush flowers are a favored source of nectar for a number of pollinator species. *Photo by Susan P. Gateley.*

Occasionally, when a lakeshore marsh breaks through its barrier bar in the spring, you may be fortunate to observe the movement of fish from the lake into the warm waters of the marsh. Alewives; suckers; and big, brawny carp may re-create the fish runs of old described in the *Jesuit Relations*, a collection of reports sent by missionaries back to their superiors in France in the 1600s. Carp are especially determined and will power up an outlet barely deep enough to wet their tummies. A lot of people look down on carp, but you have to admire their sheer vitality during the spring spawning season.

Carp came to America around 1830 and were subsequently widely stocked by the U.S. Fish Commission. It was a well-meaning gesture, but many people today wish it hadn't been done. Carp tear up vegetation attractive to many native fishes. As they root around and suck up the bottom filtering out food items, carp muddy the water, driving away sight-feeders like the pike and walleye. While many anglers dislike carp, the fish does have its supporters. Carp are respected in Asia for their strength, and a few anglers actually enjoy catching them. If you do manage to hook one, it'll put up a furious fight.

I'm not a big fan of carp at the dinner table, but I do like to watch them in the water. They are big and active, and when they enter the shallows to spawn, they're very accessible for fish watching. I can't say that they are as pretty as a shiny, streamlined silver salmon, but, by golly, they are tough.

Carp enter weedy shallows and the fringes of cattail marshes to spawn when the water warms up to around sixty-two degrees. Carp are normally very suspicious and cautious, but when the passion to reproduce warms their blood, they throw caution to the wind and try to jam themselves into all sorts of shallows and cul-de-sacs. They thrash and splash and fling their eggs about with gay abandon in the hopes that they will stick to underwater vegetation and submerged sticks and objects.

One summer, the usual gang was banging and wallowing and thrashing furiously in Main Duck's little anchorage when we took a walk along its shore. The water was high that year, and in spots our path was just about awash. Ahead we saw something sort of like a football lying in the middle of the road. When we got closer, we saw it was a sizeable carp, stranded and hard aground. It was still gulping but was none too lively, so I decided to try to shove the fish back into the pond. It took some effort, but we finally got it afloat, and the near-victim of unbridled passion swam slowly away, still a little woozy from its almost having "drowned" in air.

Turtle Island

The snapping turtle is another despised resident of the marsh that could use a little help these days. Until about twenty years ago, I, like almost everybody else I knew, thought snapping turtles were nasty, dangerous creatures to be avoided or killed. The only virtue of a snapper was as the main ingredient for turtle soup. Last spring, my next-door neighbor, who lives next to a large marsh, found a big one settling in for an egg-laying session in his garden. He killed it.

One day, I went wading in a small, muddy pond in search of frogs to photograph. As a child, I had been told to stay out of our creek if a snapper was sighted, as it would attack me and bite off a toe or a finger. On this spring afternoon, squishing around barefoot in the pond, I did encounter a snapper. I nearly stepped on it. The turtle gave me a casual look and moved a few inches aside and then ignored me and my bare toes.

The snapper, ironically New York's official reptile, is one of our most persecuted animals. Every spring, I see crushed, mangled snappers on country roads. Almost certainly some were hit deliberately, as they're often accused of eating ducks, gamefish and other animals considered valuable. The urge to "save" them by moving them off the pavement is pretty strong for those motorists who admire these ancient survivors. However, they demand respect and can be dangerous on land, where they are themselves at risk. A couple of summers ago, I tried to carefully put a garden shovel under one to push it out of the middle of the road. The turtle did not want to be pushed. She jumped six inches in the air, spun around to face me and hissed defiantly before scuttling across the road in about three seconds. I had no idea turtles could move like that. Another time, I picked up a small one by its tail and moved it. This, I now know, is not proper turtle rescue procedure. You can injure the animal by carrying it this way. Likewise, don't push or drag one across the rough pavement with a shovel or a stick, as you might scrape its legs. Sometimes, it's best to just leave them alone. Because I've seen so many crushed by cars, this is hard to do. In a Canadian study on a wildlife refuge, 2 percent of the drivers who saw the turtle (a model, we assume) tried to hit it. And when you do shift one out of the road, you always

Every spring, snappers like this one appear along roadsides near marshlands, where the road shoulder gravel tempts them to try digging a nest. *Photo by Susan P. Gateley.*

Snapping turtles are mild-mannered when in the water. Some are said to be able to recognize individual human faces. *Photo by Susan P. Gateley.*

drive off wondering if it will stay safe. They may very well have other ideas about where they should be—quite possibly, it's on the other side of the road from where you just left them.

Northern snappers are long-lived if they avoid autos; they can survive for fifty years or more. Unfortunately, some populations have declined sharply. Considering the alarming numbers of various turtle species—including snappers—being exported to China as food these days (thirty-two million animals were shipped there between 2003 and 2005), this decline is not reassuring. Many creatures prey on the buried eggs and just-emerged hatchlings, so snapper populations may be slow to rebuild once they are removed from pond or marsh.

The native people around the lake refer to North America as Turtle Island. Turtle, they say, swims in a primal ocean carrying the world on its back. Making eye contact with an old, mossy snapper floating alongside your boat gives one the distinct impression of their intelligence. It's not hard at all to see where reverence for this ancient beast came from. They truly do seem to be wise old citizens of the water world. They outlasted the dinosaurs. I hope they survive humans.

9

THE MOONEYE AND THE KING

When I was a child wading around on the slippery rocks of our neighborhood swim beach, a pervasive flotsam of small, dead fish onshore and in the water was a constant of summer. These, I was told, were mooneyes—tens of thousands of them, all in various stages of decomposition. Naturally, I wondered what killed them. Being six years old and a little short in the deductive reasoning department, I had no hesitation about going for a swim among the thick litter of floating fish corpses. The lake looked OK to me, even if it was killing zillions of fish.

It was a few years before I learned that the "mooneye" was more correctly known as an alewife. (The lake's true native mooneye is basically extinct now.) And a few more years passed before I learned why the alewives were dying. The alewife (*Alosa psuedoharengus*) is a herring-like fish that is not native to Lake Ontario. It lives in the open Atlantic but comes into fresh water each spring to spawn. No one knows for sure how they got into Lake Ontario. They have been here at least since the 1880s, when they were called shadines, but they have never really been happy about life in the lake. Alewives in their native marine habitat run up East Coast rivers and streams each spring seeking ponds in which to spawn. Marine alewives are respectable, plump fish that grow to between twelve and sixteen inches in length. Our scrawny Lake Ontario versions are considerably smaller, because they reside in fresh water for their whole lives, at a heavy metabolic cost to their overall size and fitness. The lake's alewives being chronically stressed, they frequently suffer from massive die-offs, often after they experience abrupt seasonal temperature changes, especially when moving inshore to spawn.

For many years after their arrival, the alewife population was held in check by the lake's larger predators, such as the Atlantic salmon, the lake trout and the now-vanished blue pike. In the nineteenth century, at least, they seemed to have little impact on the lake's overall ecology. But in the 1950s and '60s, when overfishing, increasing pollution and predation by the sea lamprey further depressed populations of the lake's few remaining top-level predator fish, the alewife population exploded, and those infamous and smelly mass die-offs of the 1960s began.

Each spring, when the lake's water warms, alewives, like many of the lake's native fishes, seek warm, protected nursery areas to spawn. By May or June, they are running up streams and entering bays and shallows. Once or twice I've seen a few of the little fish doing their circular dance of procreation in a harbor backwater, but generally they're most active after dark, when you may hear the constant swish of active spawning near the shore. Young fish feed on zooplankton, and by mid- to late August they are about two inches long. They then begin to gather into large schools to move offshore. On my home waters of Little Sodus Bay, I often see a gathering of hundreds of terns and gulls feeding on the schools of little fish as they begin heading out into open water. For a day or two, the bay is filled with noisy birds; dozens of satiated gulls sit on the water, too stuffed to fly until you nearly run them over with your boat. Then, just as suddenly as they appear, the little fish vanish. Alewives don't tolerate water colder than three degrees Celsius, so they seek out deeper areas of the lake with slightly higher temperatures in which to spend the winter.

The alewife is a filter feeder that strains zooplankton from the water with its gill rakers—a small-scale version of the baleen whales. But as they grow to adulthood, alewives also prey on individual food items, including just-hatched larval fish of various species. By the 1960s, alewives totally dominated the unbalanced lake ecosystem. Other native bait fishes—the lake herring, the cisco and the yellow perch—lost out as the alewife eliminated them, partly by feeding on their young and partly by outcompeting them for zooplankton. By 1965, biologists estimated that the alewife made up 90 percent of the total biomass of Lake Michigan's fish population. They also dominated Lakes Ontario, Erie and Huron.

While today it's rare to see even a few dead alewives littering the water, in the 1960s, when the vast schools of little silver fish moved inshore in late spring to spawn, they experienced massive mortalities on encountering the warm shallows. The abrupt change in temperature shocked their systems, and the already stressed six-inch fish died by the zillions. On some beaches,

Young-of-the-year alewife (about two inches long) found in the bottom of my dinghy late last summer. *Photo by Susan P. Gateley*.

waves piled up their carcasses in windrows a foot thick and ten feet wide. In the record-setting die-off of the summer of 1967, the city of Wilmette on Lake Michigan hauled sixty tons of fish off one beach in just two days. The buzzing swarms of flies and the stench of putrid flesh rotting under the summer sun put a decided damper on the beach crowds and the hot dog and lemonade business at concession stands. "Do something," said the mayors, tourist agency executives, waterfront homeowners and swimmers who were tired of stinking beaches.

Perhaps because of the large population of beach users at Lake Michigan's south end, the lake's fishery department was the first to experiment successfully with establishing a salmon-stocking program to reduce alewife populations. In 1966, after a control program for the destructive sea lamprey was established, a batch of coho salmon was planted in the lake. Within a couple of years, splendid silver salmon weighing twenty pounds were striking the anglers' lures, and the fishery boomed. Before long, fishery managers on the other Great Lakes also began stocking salmon, and anglers were coming to the Great Lakes from hundreds of miles away to catch forty pounders. Other nonnative salmon and trout—brown trout originally from Europe, steelhead trout from the West Coast and various hybrids—were also stocked to diversify the fishery and extend its season. They collectively made short work of the alewife surplus.

King salmon. *Photo by Nick Longrich.*

The chinook, or king salmon, was, in this novel new fishery, the big draw. It's the largest of the Pacific salmon species. Saltwater fish weighing over one hundred pounds have been landed. On Lake Ontario, the current record for a chinook salmon is forty-seven pounds. After being stocked as fingerlings, they spend several years in the lake eating their favorite food, the alewife. Then, one late-summer day, ancient urges begin to drive the big silver fish to move from the open lake into its nearshore waters to seek a suitable spawning stream. We have few fast-flowing, cool, clean rivers big enough to accommodate them on the south shore, and the larger tributaries like the Oswego and Genesee have dams or waterfalls that block the fish from suitable spawning areas. However, at the lake's east end, the well-named Salmon River does offer spawning grounds below the lower reservoir dam. The fish run there peaks in October. The salmon don't feed much while in the river, but they will strike a lure, so anglers come from all over the Northeast and even from abroad to try for a fifty pounder.

The king salmon is a one-shot wonder when it comes to spawning. After the eggs are fertilized, both male and female fish die, and their bodies quickly decay to feed the stream and its varied life, including the larval salmon that hatch a few months later. A well-established population of king salmon in Lake Ontario spawns successfully in several New York and Canadian lake tributaries, including the Salmon River, where a popular fishery in the downstream stretch of the river exists for them. Some of the fish running upstream through Pulaski are diverted into the New York State–run hatchery at Altmar. Here, eggs and milt are collected, eggs are fertilized and the hatched fry are raised to fingerling size for stocking in the lake the next spring.

The salmon spawning run also attracts the attention of another sleek West Coast native, the steelhead trout. Like the salmon, they spend their adult lives in the open lake but move into the streams in the fall and later in the winter to spawn. While in the river, they also gobble up any available salmon eggs and provide anglers with more excitement.

After the stocking program got underway, the hungry salmon and trout soon cleaned up the excess alewives. The multimillion-dollar recreational fishery continues to this day. (The sea lamprey's impact on the Great Lakes fisheries is another story. It has been told in several books. We will just say here that it was control of this creature that made the new fishery possible and that some believe it was human action rather than the sea lamprey that devastated our historical fisheries.)

At the same time that the various nonnative salmonids were being stocked, efforts were underway to bring back the lake's native top predators, the lake trout and the Atlantic salmon. Neither species was as quick to reestablish itself in the lake, however, as the West Coast salmon and trout were. Natural reproduction of the lake trout in the open waters of Ontario was inhibited by alewives, which gobbled up just-hatched baby trout on the spawning reefs. And the nonnative salmon were far more popular among the anglers than were the lake trout.

The coho and king salmon and the steelhead and brown trout grow fast, get big and are more fun to catch than are lake trout. The popular king salmon also feeds almost exclusively on alewives in Lake Ontario, unlike the lake trout, which spends more time near the lake bottom devouring a variety of food items. King salmon grow to thirty pounds in just a few years on a diet of alewives. Indeed, they have been so successful at gobbling up the once-superabundant "mooneye" that a pending shortage of alewives has prompted recent reductions in the stocking rates of kings.

Unfortunately, neither of the lake's native open lake predators, the lake trout and the Atlantic salmon, thrives on a steady diet of alewives. Alewife tissue contains an enzyme that breaks down thiamine, an important vitamin for the development of eggs and young fish. When Atlantic salmon and lake

Stringer of trophy salmon from Lake Ontario. *Photo from Werner Stenger.*

trout eat a steady diet of alewives, they suffer a vitamin deficiency that affects their reproduction. After their eggs hatch, the tiny fry go belly-up within a few days with something the hatchery folk called "Cayuga Syndrome" before they knew the cause of mortality. This unhealthy attribute of alewife diets has prompted an effort to reestablish in Lake Ontario native bait fish like the cisco, a species the laker evolved with and does well on as a food fish.

Some observers have said that fishery managers should put more effort into the restoration of the original naturally reproducing, top-level predators of our lake rather than depending on hatchery production. But as one biologist told a meeting with anglers in early 2020, "You are never going to bring back the fish community of two centuries ago." The various species of small bait fish—those ciscoes, chubs, shiners and sculpins of the nineteenth century that the native trout and salmon fed on—have dwindled in number or vanished completely from Lake Ontario. Some of the various races of lake herring are now extinct. Some believe that too many other aspects of our ecosystem, including the watershed of the lake, have changed for full restoration of our native fish community to be possible. Many anglers seeking a trophy fish want the exciting battle with a spectacular, hard-fighting Pacific salmon. As one told me, bringing in a native lake trout is like reeling in an old boot. And because anglers pay the license fees that keep the hatcheries operating and the state's fishery managers paid, there will always be a bias toward maintaining a big, fun sport fishery based largely on hatchery-raised salmon and trout.

However, many observers feel that a more diverse array of bait fish in the lake would be beneficial to all of the various species of sport fish and that nature's resiliency is not to be underestimated. As we shall see in the last chapter, nature may have its own ideas about the future of the lake's fishery. Some of the lake's natives continue to survive in remnant populations. About ten years ago, efforts got underway to restore the cisco, a species of native lake herring, and another, similar fish, the bloater, in Ontario by stocking young hatchery-raised fish in the hope of establishing self-sustaining populations. Eggs were obtained from a population of fish that still comes inshore to spawn each fall in Chaumont Bay, and young fish were raised in a federal hatchery facility. When they reached fingerling size, they were released in Irondequoit and Sodus Bays. The bloater, another species of lake herring that spends much of its life in deep water, has also been raised and released in several areas along the lakeshore.

Many of Lake Ontario's salmon and trout, like these in the Altmar hatchery fishway, begin their lives in hatchery tanks. *Photo by Susan P. Gateley.*

Besides being compatible with the nutrition requirements of the lake's native lakers and Atlantic salmon, the cisco and bloater are not subject to the winter and spring die-off problems that the alewife suffers from. Bringing them back into the lake's food web could increase the overall resilience of an ecosystem that has been greatly modified and simplified since the days when the Haudenosaunee fished our south-shore bays and rivers.

A cottage industry of small charter fishing vessels now generates a considerable part of the estimated annual $7 billion revenue generated by the Great Lakes recreational fishery. On Lake Ontario's New York shore, dozens of charter captains take anglers out on the lake in quest of a thirty-pound trophy. They typically employ owner-operated boats twenty-five to thirty feet in size, often with twin engines and equipped with enough high-tech digital and electronic gear to keep a full-time technician busy. Equipment aboard twenty-first-century sport-fishing boats includes GPS and chart plotters, digital fish finders with side scan and down view sonar integrated with mapping software, thermal sensing units and more. Many of the charter boats have a half-dozen electric downriggers costing several hundred dollars apiece along with multidirectional rod holders and dozens of colorful, shiny fishing lures at $8 or $10 each. Then there's downrigger weights, planer boards, rods and reels and the usual boating gear, including radar. And don't forget the GoPro camera so you can take underwater video of the action to promote your business on Facebook. Put it all together, and if the package includes a fairly new boat and motor and a shiny truck to tow it all home at the end of the season, the endeavor easily comes to six figures. But if your customers drive hundreds of miles and pay for accommodations plus perhaps $600 or more for the half-day charter to catch a king, reliable state-of-the-art gear is essential for the operation to make money during the all-too-short season (April to October).

Given the amount of electronics and software required to manage all this high-tech equipment, it's little wonder that the fishing guide works "the back of the boat" while the mate steers the craft, taking care to avoid entanglements with other charter boats and their gear. Still, once the king hits, it's man versus fish in a duel that hasn't changed a whole lot since Isasac Walton's day. For the most part, charter captains try to avoid rough weather on their deepwater trips in the summer, but when the fish are widely scattered, they may have to run five or ten miles offshore. Even at planing speeds, it can take them nearly an hour to get back to the dock if bad weather threatens. The lake can kick up three- to four-foot waves in far less time than that.

Anglers from Massachusetts, Pennsylvania, New Jersey and other areas travel from hundreds of miles away to book salmon fishing charters on Lake Ontario. *Photo from Werner Stenger.*

One captain told me that, although his thirty-foot boat is heavier than most of the vessels in the local charter fleet and rides six-foot waves with ease, he tries not to go out in waves that are much over four feet. If it gets too rough, there's no way you can land the fish even if you do manage to hook one. As he put it, "When the boat's stern sinks into the trough and you have to reach up into the oncoming wave to net the fish, then it's time to go back into the bay!"

Watching the big gray salmon fight their way up the rapids and riffles of the river that runs through Pulaski on a crisp fall day evokes much of the same fascination and delight that the early settlers to our region must have felt seeing hordes of salmon running upstream. The powerful fish swimming against the relentless current are urged by age-old instinct to carry on their race. They seem like the embodiment of the river's water itself somehow made living. They may not be native to the lake, but for the time being they have adapted to it with spectacular success.

Although many problems remain, our Great Lake has come a long way since the 1960s, when the most abundant life form on its summer beaches was the buzzing swarm of blowflies hanging around the dead alewives. The

For a thousand years, anglers have come to the Salmon River at the east end of Lake Ontario, where the big fish still run each fall. *Photo by Susan P. Gateley.*

massive imbalances of the past have been reduced, at least for now, though they have not been fully corrected by the introduction of the hatchery-raised West Coast predator fish. And some of the lake's native fish and birds, like the sturgeon, the bald eagle and the osprey, are reappearing, though other members of the lake's web of life, like the once-abundant native clams and various small inshore fishes, continue to dwindle in number. Read on for a couple more success stories and a speculative peak at the future history of the lake.

RESTORATION, REDEMPTION AND RESILIENCE

When I was growing up in the 1950s, a great blue heron was a rare and thrilling sight. Today, it's rare to paddle a lakeshore tributary or marsh without seeing one. But sixty years ago, fish-eating birds of all sorts were struggling to survive on Lake Ontario, because persistent toxic pesticides like DDT, PCBs and Mirex were accumulating in the food chain. In some cases, the pesticides caused outright poisoning. Fish like the bullhead and the white sucker, which spent much of their life in contact with contaminated sediment, developed tumors and lesions; other fish that had ingested toxins in their diets showed liver damage when autopsied in the lab. When fish-eating gulls, herons or eagles laid their eggs, the various fat-soluable chemicals like Mirex and PCBs in their bodies were passed on to the egg yolks and the developing embryos. Most eggs failed to hatch. DDT, an endocrine-system disrupter that scrambles the metabolic process of calcium transport in birds, also causes abnormal egg-shell development. Often, eggs broke under the incubating mother bird.

Many toxins that ended up in the lake's sediments are still causing mutations. Back in 2006 and again in 2011, while beachcombing, I noticed wingless and deformed flies associated with dead fish. The fly maggots had failed to transform into normal adult insects, almost certainly because of concentrated mutagens in the bodies of the fish they had ingested. Back in the 1970s, even the hardy, long-lived herring gulls on the lake were being impacted by toxic and carcinogenic chemicals. The double-crested cormorant is particularly sensitive to chemicals, and its population on the lake was down to a few dozen birds by the early 1970s.

In 1972, DDT was banned by federal legislation for most uses in the United States, and cleanup of various chemical-laced dump sites began. Within a decade, the populations of the lake's fish eaters began to rebound. Today, with the reduction of persistent toxins in the lake environment, many species of birds, including the once-rare cormorant, are thriving, much to the annoyance of anglers, who often accuse the birds of eating too many baby salmon and bass in the lake. (Studies show that the cormorant that swims and feeds underwater catches whatever is available in the three- to five-inch range. Recently on Lake Ontario, that has often been the round goby, considered to be a bass-egg-eating nuisance by many anglers.)

Around 1990, I saw my first osprey flying along the south shore of the lake. Today, I know of at least four nests within ten miles of my home. And a few years later, young, recently fledged bald eagles were regular visitors to the forested shoreline between Sodus Bay and Oswego. They were the descendants of one of the first and most successful eagle-restoration efforts made by state and federal wildlife biologists in North America.

After the ban on DDT went into effect, biologists traveled to Alaska and to several areas around the upper Great Lakes to collect recently hatched eaglets. These they brought to the Montezuma National Wildlife Refuge, about twenty miles south of Lake Ontario. The young birds were placed on "hacking" platforms and fed by people who concealed themselves from the nestlings. This hacking technique has been used for many years by falconers to raise young hawks and to sharpen their hunting prowess. The baby eagles were monitored by a camera, and after they fledged, biologists continued to place fish (mostly carp from the nearby Cayuga Seneca Canal that borders the marsh) on the platform. The first hand-reared birds "graduated" in 1976. Four years later, a nest near the east end of Lake Ontario was seen with a pair of banded birds that had come from the program. By 1988, enough eagles had survived and established nests to shut down the hacking program. Today, the DEC estimates that there are perhaps five hundred active nests statewide, including dozens along the south shore of Lake Ontario.

Each year since the mid-1990s, I've seen the dark-brown juveniles show up around the end of July at a forested bluff near Port Bay to practice their soaring skills. On days when a brisk north or northwest wind prevails, the birds ride updrafts off the eighty-foot bluff as they glide back and forth along the edge of the lake.

Sometimes they descend to within thirty feet of the shore in front of a small creek and hover on outstretched wings over a beach walker, seemingly curious about the two-legged critter below. I once watched a youngster try to land on a tree branch. He grabbed the branch but then lost his balance and flipped upside down. After some flapping, the bird managed to right himself. I've also seen the young birds occasionally make grabs at each other with their talons, turning on their backs as they do so. The adult eagle mating ritual involves similar moves in a spectacular display in which the two birds approach each other in flight and lock their talons together to "swing your partner." They then spiral downward, whirling around each other for hundreds of feet before disengaging. It's a maneuver that obviously takes practice by the youngsters. By September, the juveniles begin to disperse from the area they were raised in.

Big trees are an important part of the birds' habitat, as eagles need perches on leafless tree limbs along the bluff edge to survey the lake for fish dinners. They also keep an eye out for a passing osprey carrying a fish. Eagles and ospreys don't get along—the bigger, stronger eagle will rob an osprey of its meal any chance it gets. If an eagle sees an osprey with a fish, it usually takes off and chases the hapless osprey, trying to make it drop its catch.

Despite its less-than-honorable code of ethics toward neighboring fish hawks, the bald eagle is a marvel to watch in flight. The seven-foot wingspan and overall size is amazing when seen close up. I've stood on a

Bald eagles typically pair off for life. *Photo by Susan P. Gateley.*

bluff edge a few times and watched an eagle fly by at eye level a few yards offshore. The birds sometimes turn their heads to examine me, making eye contact as they glide by.

I've watched them dozens of times swoop down to the water and snatch at the surface, only to come up empty. A couple of times I have seen an eagle actually catch a fish. Though fish is their preferred food, they are opportunistic and will kill and eat other birds and animals up to the size of an adult rabbit. They also eat carrion, and I've encountered them more than once in early spring by the roadside on a dead deer or raccoon.

Unlike the eagle, the osprey, another big fish-eating bird, made it back to Lake Ontario on its own. Ospreys are distributed across much of the Great Lakes region (as well as on New York's saltwater coast). I first encountered them on the Chesapeake Bay, where, in the 1970s, their large, messy nests were a familiar sight perched atop various navigation aids and light beacons. They showed up on Lake Ontario in the mid-1980s, and there are now at least 150 active nests in the Finger Lakes region. Ospreys seem to be more tolerant of human disturbances than are bald eagles when nesting. One survey found nine out of ten nests were built on man-made structures. The first nest I saw near Lake Ontario was on a big factory chimney, and I've seen a nest atop a lighting structure at a high school athletic field. The most favored site for a nest around my neighborhood is on the cross-arms of a utility pole. National Grid was kind enough to put a platform up for a pair of birds near my home, even as it installed anti-bird spikes on the utility pole the birds insisted on using. It took a season to convince them, but since then, the pair has been happily raising chicks for the last four years on their custom-built platform.

It makes for good public relations as well as economic sense for the utility companies to offer safe nesting alternatives. Once in a while, a nesting osprey using a utility pole manages to create a short circuit, getting fried and causing a power outage in the process. The internet reports that more than one nest of dry sticks have caught fire, sometimes burning the utility pole with it.

One of the more spectacular courtship displays you may be lucky enough to see along the lake shore is the osprey's "sky dance." During the display, the male swoops, hovers and peeps to show off his manly strength and aerial abilities to a prospective mate. You can often observe osprey behavior quite easily from your car or boat without disturbing the birds.

Ospreys appear to be better fishermen than bald eagles. More than once I've seen an eagle or a couple of big gulls chase an osprey to steal its catch.

Osprey considering the suitability of a man-made nest platform. *Photo by Susan P. Gateley.*

At least some of the time, despite being loaded down with a fish, the osprey escapes. Last fall, we were sailing along the shore with a brisk southerly wind on flat water when we saw an osprey flying very low over the water. We were probably two miles off Sodus Bay, and the bird was hauling a big bass, not a fish commonly associated with the open lake. He or she seemed to be on course to intercept us. After crossing our bow, the osprey rose to about twenty feet and hovered briefly over the stern of the boat, apparently debating whether to try landing on it. The bird decided not to try and turned back toward the distant land, again flying low and skimming the water. We speculated that the bird been chased offshore by an eagle and was getting pretty tired of carrying that big fish and was hoping for a rest stop. (Our boat at anchor has in the past served as a perch for ospreys.)

It takes the birds most of the summer to raise their chicks, and much of the fishing is done by the male while his mate tends the kids, sheltering them with her wings from blistering heat or from rain. By August, though, she begins leaving them alone and joins the male in hunting for food for the nearly grown young. Toward the end of the summer, on a breezy day you may see a young bird hanging on to the edge of the nest or perhaps jumping up and down as he flaps his wings. Then, one day, it launches off into the unknown. According to the literature, the young are fed by the parents for

After one season, this mother osprey left this nest and opted for the nearby nest platform provided by the utility company. *Photo by Susan P. Gateley.*

several weeks after fledging but then manage to instinctively pick up the skills needed to catch fish on their own.

The adults leave for the sunny south at summer's end before the youngsters do. Last year, we watched the single chick of a pair hang around Little Sodus Bay for a week or two before it headed off, perhaps to Brazil. Young ospreys do not return to North America the following spring. They remain behind while the adults head north. If they survive the trip south, they spend a year and a half in South America and return, often to the area they grew up in, to seek a mate.

Some years ago, a female osprey was captured at the Montezuma Refuge south of Lake Ontario and fitted with a radio transmitter that could be monitored by satellite. She left the refuge on August 26 and followed the Appalachian Mountains south to Florida, arriving on September 6. She then crossed the Caribbean to Cuba and went on to the Dominican Republic. After that, she reached the islands off the coast of Venezuela, taking two days to cross open water nonstop. She arrived in Venezuela on September 18 and then slowly continued on to spend the winter in the heart of Brazil on the Amazon River.

GOOSE SUCCESS STORY

One of the most ubiquitous waterfowl around the lake's bays, marshes and other protected waters is the Canada goose. It wasn't always so. Forty years ago, the only Canada geese I ever saw near Lake Ontario were migrants, high in the sky heading south or north in their characteristic *V* formation. But today, they are a common sight in the summer, grazing on or lounging about the parks, golf courses and waterfront lawns of the lake's heavily built-up bays. Geese, unlike most of North America's waterfowl, have benefited from man's activities, as they thrive on a diet largely consisting of grass.

Before World War II, most of Lake Ontario's geese were migratory. But starting in the 1950s, a number of programs were started in New York and elsewhere to reintroduce Canada geese to areas where they had become scarce. Sportsmen's clubs and other organizations imported geese from the upper Midwest, home to a so-called giant race of the birds. The descendants of these nonmigratory "resident" geese have since prospered in a man-made landscape of commodity cornfields and residential lawns. They have done so well that many waterfront homeowners consider them pests.

It's said that a goose poops every twenty minutes. They certainly are very good at rapidly processing the tender new grass of a well-manicured lawn. And the short grass and open spaces of a big lawn feel secure to the geese as they keep a constant lookout for concealed predators. People object to messes in their yards, and large populations of geese can pollute the water with coliform bacteria. Having said that, the entertainment value of these strong-flying honkers has earned them many admirers. One survey on the coast showed about three-quarters of the population liked having them around in parks and public spaces.

Geese can live up to twenty-five years in the wild and mate for life around age three. They build nests in marshes and near the water and often use a grassy hummock or a muskrat lodge as a base. The goose lays up to eight eggs and does most of the sitting while the gander stands guard. The baby goslings hatch after about four weeks of incubation. Because the embryos don't develop until all of the eggs are laid and incubation begins, they all hatch at once. Within a day or two, they're eating tender grass by the road or in someone's yard and swimming close astern of their parents.

Geese are quite territorial during nesting, and they maintain social distancing as a family unit after the babies hatch. I often see geese swimming around with a parent at each end of the line of fluffy babies. When they get near another family, there's usually some head bobbing, and sometimes nasty

Canada geese, like bald eagles, typically pair off for life. *Photo by Susan P. Gateley.*

things are said. Yet, oddly enough, I've also seen mixed groups of different-sized babies being looked after by a guardian goose. These so-called gang broods can consist of several dozen goslings all gathered under the watchful eye of a single parent. A recent photo posted online showed a goose followed by no less than forty-seven babies.

The fuzzy, golden goslings grow incredibly fast. By midsummer, when they're two to three months old, they're out on the water taking flying lessons, flapping along on short, low flights. Within days, they're pros at it, and the family units begin to blend into larger flocks. Geese are powerful fliers, averaging about forty miles an hour when underway on a long passage. Migrating birds have been known to cover 1,500 miles in a day if they get a boost from a tailwind. They've been seen at altitudes of nearly two miles. However, most of the geese we see around the lakeshore and in the bays and marshes are nonmigratory and spend the winter working local cornfields for waste grain if the snow isn't too deep and feeding in ice-free shallows. They stick together as a family through the winter before the young birds go off to find mates and start their own families.

The internet says that goose pairs form strong bonds and have a low divorce rate. But I once saw an interesting "interracial" marriage between a

Geese and mute swans overwinter near food supplies furnished by ice-free shallows like those of the Pond at Fair Haven's state park. *Photo by Susan P. Gateley.*

Canada gander and a domestic graylag-type goose. She had been dumped in Pultneyville's harbor one fall and joined the resident mallard duck flock, surviving through the winter on handouts of cracked corn. In the spring, a Canada goose started hanging out with her. Perhaps he was a widower. He soon taught her how to fly, something we hadn't seen her do at all during the previous fall and winter. As spring moved on, the birds built a nest right in front of the floating dock where I kept my boat.

For several weeks, I edged around the nest in an uneasy truce with the pair. The gander hissed and threatened but let me sneak by. Then one day, he assaulted me full-on and gave me a sharp pinch on the back of my leg. We cussed each other out, and the next day, the nest was empty. I suspect the babies were just about to hatch, making the father extravigilant. Hybrids of Canada and domestic geese are far from unknown, and certainly this couple produced a successful brood, for they were part of the harbor scene for several months.

In recent years, a second goose species, the snow goose, has been appearing in our skies over the lake. Snow geese are strictly migratory and pass through our area each spring and fall en route to winter grounds in Maryland and Delaware salt-marsh areas and farm fields, where they fatten on waste grain. Since the 1960s, there has been a dramatic increase in the

Snow geese now stop over in fields near Lake Ontario during migration in increasing numbers. *Photo by Susan P. Gateley*.

population of these beautiful white birds with their black-tipped wings. The Atlantic flyway population once was estimated at about fifty thousand birds. Today, it's estimated to be closer to one million. Because of concerns that the geese are overgrazing their northern breeding grounds, hunters in the Finger Lakes region are allowed to shoot up to twenty-five snow geese a day during the season.

AN ANCIENT SURVIVOR MAKES A COMEBACK

Of all the lake's fishes, only the lamprey has a more ancient lineage than the sturgeon. And individual fish can also be ancient. It's believed that female lake sturgeon can live up to 150 years. The notion of a fish swimming our waters as a juvenile during the 1901 Pan-American Exposition in Buffalo or during the Great Gale of 1880 on Lake Ontario is more than a little mind-boggling. But once the fish get to a certain size (and lake sturgeon can grow to three hundred pounds and six feet in length), they have no natural predators. Only humans can tackle these giants.

Several features mark the sturgeon as a primitive fish similar to those that swam waters of the world 250 million years ago during the Triassic period. Its body is covered by a bony armor of flat plates called scutes, while much of its skeleton is made of cartilage, a feature it shares with the shark family. Sturgeon have other shark-like features, like their asymmetric tail fin. The lake sturgeon is a bottom feeder and spends much of its time in nearshore waters at depths of thirty feet or less. It has four sensory whiskers, somewhat like those of a catfish, that it drags through the bottom mud in search of small food items, including crayfish, clams, zebra mussels and insect larvae. One study of sturgeon in Wisconsin found that the fish lived almost exclusively on midge larvae sucked up from the bottom.

Long-lived sturgeon don't begin to reproduce until they are well into their teenage years. Then, spawning is often an every-other-year affair. The big fish historically ran up rivers like the Genesee and Oswego to spawn over beds of clean gravel underlying well-oxygenated flowing water. Sometimes, they also used wave-washed rock ledges near the shore for spawning grounds. The young grew rapidly after hatching, sometimes measuring six inches in their first year, and tagging studies suggest that some ranged widely throughout the lake before returning to their birthplace to spawn as fifteen- to twenty-year-old fish. Unfortunately, the sturgeon is now exceedingly rare in Lake Ontario. Pollution, overfishing and the construction of dams that blocked spawning runs all contributed to its demise.

Surprisingly, this source of prized caviar and high-quality flesh was once considered a "trash fish." Big sturgeon lumbering along the bottom would get tangled up in nets set for perch or bullhead and would then thrash their way out, tearing up and tangling the gear as they did so. Because no local market then existed for caviar, they were often killed and dumped back in the lake. There are tales of sturgeon being hauled out and stacked onshore to dry. Their oil-rich bodies were then burned as fuel in steamer boilers.

Lake sturgeon, despite their great size and age, feed low on the lake's food chain. *Wikipedia.*

Other early accounts of the Lake Ontario fishery recall sturgeon being fed to pigs or used as fertilizer on the fields.

The native peoples here, however, prized the sturgeon, whose meat was well suited to smoking and/or drying and salting. Mishe-Nahme, the "king of fishes," as Longfellow calls the sturgeon in the *Song of Hiawatha*, was a vital part of their diet throughout the region. The fish was also important to their culture. For many First Nations folk, sturgeon hold spiritual significance. To those who follow the clan system, members of the sturgeon clan are considered to be mediators and teachers. The deliberate dignity and calm way of these ancients as they forage for food in the shallows perhaps inspired clan members to seek wisdom and patience. Sturgeon clan people help children develop skills and healthy spirits and are peacemakers who solve disputes among clans.

The native people built weirs of stone in rivers to divert and concentrate spring-run sturgeon as they traveled upstream to spawn. The Seneca Band used large rakes to drive them into the weir "pocket," where they could then spear them. Other Indian bands harpooned them from canoes, according to Charlevoix. Bone harpoon heads have been found in considerable numbers at sites around Chaumont Bay and by the outlets of Oneida Lake at Brewerton and at Onondaga Lake. In New England, Indians used torches to light up the shallows at night and attract sturgeon inshore to be speared. It seems likely that tribes here sometimes used similar techniques. Lafitau, in the *Jesuit Relations*, recalls: "The meat of the sturgeon was preserved by smoking. During the summer, they [the lodges] are cool enough, but full of fleas and bedbugs, and stink very badly when they [the Indians] dry their fish in the smoke."

Eventually, the Europeans came to share the native views of the sturgeon. After the advent of rail transport in the 1870s, it was possible to quickly move goods to distant markets. This brought about the rise of large-scale commercial fishing, and the once-scorned sturgeon was sought after for its firm oily flesh and for a material called isinglass that was made from dried swim bladders. Among its other uses, brewers employed isinglass to accelerate the clarification of beer. In the 1920s, in harbors like Pultneyville and Sodus Bay, sturgeon were caught on trot lines and held in pens until enough were on hand for a butchering day. Then the iced fish were transported to a nearby rail station and sent off to downstate markets.

Very quickly after commercial fishing for them began, the sturgeon population dwindled. These long-lived fish grow slowly. Though a large fish may produce half a million eggs, either the vast majority of these are eaten before hatching or the tiny fish are eaten by predators. It takes several years for a baby sturgeon to become too big for other fish to gobble up.

Along with overfishing, dams and pollution were other major contributors to the population decline. When sturgeon runs were blocked by dams, the clean gravel and rubble and flowing water needed for egg survival was no longer available for them. The fish that spawned in the open lake shallows also had to contend with changes in the shoreline habitat. As pollution from sewage and other sources added nutrients to the lake, "sea weed" (a filamentous algae called *Cladophora*) began to cover the rocks with a dense growth that may have suffocated the deposited eggs. The little remaining river habitat for spawning and nursery areas still existing below dams was often degraded by dredging and additional pollution.

Any fish that escaped natural hazards were eagerly sought by fishermen. In the 1920s, a major source of caviar for European markets was our own lake sturgeon. Today, smoked sturgeon goes for $70 a pound, so a one-hundred-pound fish adds up to real money. Caviar, the unspawned salted eggs of the sturgeon, recently was bringing up to $100 an ounce, so the eggs of a large fish would be worth six figures on the retail market. Not surprisingly, poaching on the Great Lakes is a problem, and one recent scientific study of St. Lawrence River spawning had the location "x'd" out, presumably to protect the vulnerable fish. A 2016 story in the *Toronto Star* stated that, by weight, the value of caviar can equal or exceed the equivalent in cocaine.

There is no legal fishing season now for sturgeon on Lake Ontario. About twenty years ago, a variety of programs got underway on several of the Great Lakes in an effort to build up the native fish population. Cleaner waters and a closed fishing season made it feasible to restore the sturgeon by stocking hatchery-raised juveniles. The restoration plan for New York included stocking five thousand young sturgeon in each of several rivers, including the Genesee, that were identified as suitable habitat.

It's a long-term project according to biologist Dawn Dittman, who writes that perhaps two generations of sturgeon (fifty years or more) will have to survive and spawn before the success of the stocking program can be determined.

To some of the original lake watchers who lived here in centuries past, the sturgeon was thought to represent wisdom. My experience in the field as a student on a sampling excursion for a small relative of the lake sturgeon, the short-nose sturgeon, left me with the distinct impression that this was a fish of great stoicism and stubborn survival. Around 1957, I stood as a child on the edge of a low bluff on the shores of Lake Ontario on a cool,

Juvenile lake sturgeon, similar to the young fish now being stocked at various points on the lake's south shore. *Photo by Susan P. Gateley.*

breezy late morning in May. I looked down at the wave-washed ledges below and was astonished to see a half-dozen huge fish thrashing around in the shallow water. I ran back to my mother to report this amazing sight. Were they dying? Were they trying to get out of the water? Would they attack me? My mother's friend, the homeowner, assured me that these were merely spawning sturgeon laying their eggs—nothing to worry about.

I don't know if I'll ever see those big fish in the wild again, but the drive to survive is strong. Many people share my desire to preserve these amazing creatures and are working to make it happen. With human help, the sturgeon could return to the lake's south-shore ledges, and those of us who watch the water may see the ancient ones again.

Humans often strive for simplified, predictable environments, like a golf course or a lawn, where no venomous snakes or stalking leopards can conceal themselves. But these landscapes of monocultural turf grass come at a price. It takes constant inputs of fossil fuel, herbicides and labor to maintain their artificial green perfection. If those inputs stop, the weeds soon begin to pop up. Queen Anne's lace and dandelions attract pollinators. Insects arrive to feed on foliage, and birds arrive to feed on insects. Before long, the lawn has become a flower-filled meadow with bees, chirping crickets and flitting butterflies. Poison ivy, mice and perhaps a toad or a snake or two may also arrive. Perhaps a squirrel starts burying nuts in the onetime lawn, and baby oaks appear.

Though we resist it with a $90 billion landscaping industry, nature's messy complexity is essential to human welfare. Even organizations like the World Bank now recognize how vital biodiversity is to our economic, psychological and cultural well-being. It is certainly true, as many experts have said, that our Great Lake will never host the abundance of native life that Charlevoix and various Jesuit missionaries documented. But with a little encouragement and a less-polluted environment, salmon again swim its waters, and eagles and ospreys again fish along its shoreline. Efforts are ongoing to bring back native fishes like the sturgeon and the cisco. As we head into the last two chapters of this work, don't give up hope!

ALIENS AMONG US

All over the world, freshwater ecosystems are in trouble. Lakes and rivers cover less than 1 percent of the world's surface, yet hundreds of the world's most endangered animals, including many species of fish, live in fresh water. Some of them, like the deepwater sculpin and the blue pike, once called Lake Ontario home. Environmental stresses from human action, including overfishing and pollution, have helped open the door to a flood of immigrant animals and plants in freshwater ecosystems worldwide. Here on the Great Lakes perhaps 180 different plant and animal exotics now reside in our waters.

Often, alien invaders, when introduced to a simplified and stressed ecosystem lacking its historic biodiversity, out-compete the lakes' remaining natives, causing further environmental damage. The system's biodiversity then decreases still more, becoming even more unstable. Once, Lake Ontario's open waters were home to a half-dozen different bait fishes, each of which lived and fed in a slightly different part of the lake. Today, one species, the alewife, makes up the vast majority of the forage fish biomass.

Perhaps the best-known recent invasive species to arrive in Lake Ontario is the zebra mussel, along with its close relative the quagga mussel. These two mollusks have completely rewoven the web of life here. They have been called ecosystem engineers, and their arrival in the Great Lakes and subsequent wide-ranging impacts led to passage of federal legislation called the National Invasive Species Act in 1996 that attempted to control and prevent further such "invasions." Since then, research has shown that nonnative aquatic plants and animals have caused billions of dollars of economic losses in the United States even as they have further destabilized our Great Lakes environment. Nonnative plants, including water chestnut, frog bit and a cattail species, along with creatures like round gobies, fishhook water fleas and even cholera bacteria, have made it into the Great Lakes.

No other alien invader has impacted Lake Ontario more than the little brown shellfish from the Caspian Sea region. They first arrived around 1988 as passengers in ship ballast tank water. A single adult mussel can produce one million eggs a year, and unlike our native clams and mussels, the zebra and quagga mussels produce larvae, called veligers, that float, allowing them to disperse rapidly. After their arrival to a place with no natural predators or other controls, the little shellfish spread like wildfire through the Great Lakes system. Within a couple of years, they had carpeted much of the bottom of Lake Ontario. Soon, windrows and piles of sun-bleached white shells up to three feet thick were appearing on lake beaches in the spring.

Since each mussel can filter a liter of water a day, and since thousands of them may crowd into a square yard of hard bottom, it's easy to see how they may impact the lake's planktonic animal and plant life as well as its clarity and chemistry. Research suggests they are able to filter the entire volume of

Ice-scoured zebra mussel shells bleached by the sun and pulverized by waves now make up white "sand" beaches on Main Duck Island in Canada. *Photo by Susan P. Gateley.*

Lake St. Clair twice a day at population densities of six thousand mussels per square meter of lake bottom. And to make matters even worse for the lake's native zooplankton and larval fishes, the mussels are picky about their food and are capable of selectively filtering out the more nutritious diatoms vital to the lake's food chain while rejecting less-tasty cyanobacteria. Researchers suspect that this selective feeding has helped fuel more frequent outbreaks of toxic pond scum on the lakes.

A major culprit in these outbreaks of hazardous algae is the one-celled organism called microcystis, which produces a potent liver toxin. Exposure to it can cause skin rashes and respiratory distress, and if ingested, it can cause liver damage in humans and other animals. Cattle and dogs have died after ingesting scum containing microcystis. An outbreak of hazardous algae consisting largely of microcystis in Lake Erie in 2014 shut down Toledo's drinking-water supply for several days. It's been estimated that increasingly hazardous algae blooms nationwide are costing more than $4 billion a year.

As the zebra and quagga mussel filter vast amounts of plankton, they also compete directly with the lake's fishes that depend on plankton as larvae and juveniles. While the filtered water looks nice and clear and clean to the casual observer, the mussels are diverting huge amounts of energy from the lake's waters to its bottom, reducing food for the open-water alewives that those trophy king salmon and trout depend on. Since the mussel infestation, fishery managers have had to reduce the numbers of hatchery-raised salmon and trout stocked because the alewife population has declined. In late 2019, they announced stocking rate cutbacks of 20 percent for the sought-after king salmon for the 2020 season.

Studies of other lakes that have been invaded by the mussels suggest that the biomass of fish those waters can support may have been reduced by up to one-third. After the zebra mussel reached Oneida Lake, walleye biomass dropped by approximately half, and first-year walleye averaged about 12 percent smaller than in the recent past. (Smaller young fish tend to have lower subsequent survival rates through their first winter.)

The greatly increased clarity of the lake's water has had another interesting and unexpected side effect. Under certain conditions, it promotes production of deadly botulism toxins that can kill fish and fish-eating birds. Now, because light penetrates much deeper into the water than in pre–zebra mussel times, far greater amounts of the filamentous green algae called *Cladophora* are able to grow on the bottom. This "seaweed," a native to the Great Lakes region, thrives in shallow, sunlit areas near shore, where it covers the rocks with a thick green pelt of "fur." Historically, it posed no problems to the environmental well-being of the lake, however, nutrient-rich runoff from farm fields and human waste disposal has fertilized its growth. When storm waves crash ashore later in the summer, they rip the excess algae growth off the bottom and carry it onto the beach. Here the rotting plants form putrid, stinking gray mats. Some of the dead algae is also moved offshore by wave action, where it lies on the bottom and rots. As it decays, it uses up oxygen. In the ensuing anaerobic environment, with no oxygen present, certain bacteria may then release "swamp gas" (methane) from the organic ooze. Sometimes, the methane gas floats gray chunks and mats of the rotted algae to the surface, where it smells like sewage. This septic environment promotes the growth of *Clostridium botulinum*, a type of bacteria that sometimes produces a potent neurotoxin deadly to vertebrates.

Clostridium botulinum is found widely in the environment. One strain is known for killing people who fail to home-can their beans and other low-acid foods correctly. The toxin is very lethal. It's said that the amount in a contaminated fly maggot's gut may be sufficient to kill an adult mallard. And in the last twenty years or so, the number of outbreaks of botulism poisoning of birds on the Great Lakes has increased.

About fifteen years ago, thousands of dead gulls, grebes, long-tailed ducks, loons and other fish-eating birds began washing up on the beaches of Lake Michigan. At the same time, a few dead round gobies, another common invasive species in Lake Ontario, also showed up on our beaches. And later that year, we, too, found dead birds washing ashore. It took investigators a while to sort through the mess, but eventually, they made the connection that the little gobies were almost certainly transferring botulism from the lake bottom to the fish-eating birds.

Round gobies are native to the same part of the world that zebra and quagga mussels came from. Like the shellfish, they, too, came to America in a ship ballast tank and by 1990 were spreading rapidly throughout the region. Anglers dislike the little bait stealers that are known to gobble up the eggs of more desirable game fish like the bass and walleye. They rarely get much bigger than about six inches and appear to be pretty useless as far as a human food source goes.

However, larger gobies can and do feed on zebra mussels, and valuable game fishes feed on gobies. Unfortunately, while the filter-feeding shellfish can concentrate *botulina* bacteria in their bodies with no ill effect, the gobies that feed on contaminated mussels may suffer from botulism. Poisoned fish probably swim erratically after ingesting the toxin before dying. Biologists theorize that these gobies were easy targets for fish-eating birds that then

This round goby is shown atop a bed of zebra mussels. Larger gobies are one of the few fish able to eat the invasive shellfish. *Wikipedia.*

were poisoned. In July 2006, I recall seeing a couple of dead gulls with the characteristic "limber neck" of a bird paralyzed by the toxin. Later that fall, hundreds of dead loons and common mergansers appeared on beaches from west of Rochester to the east end of the lake. The botulism outbreak had coincided with a southward movement of migrating loons, and it hit them hard. This was one of the biggest bird kills on Lake Ontario if not the entire state ever recorded. Thousands of loons, along with grebes, cormorants, mergansers and other fish-eaters, died that fall. The rookery on Little Galloo earlier in the summer also experienced an outbreak among its nesting terns and gulls.

Some studies suggest that botulism outbreaks may be associated with hot summers and high runoff, leading to more abundant growth of attached algae near the shore. Unfortunately, these are two factors that also contribute to hazardous toxic algae blooms, which seem to be on a general increase throughout the region.

THE WATER CHESTNUT

While many of Lake Ontario's unwanted immigrant species have arrived aboard ships, other invasives have made their way to the lake through deliberate introductions by people seeking to "improve" nature. Such was the case with a pesky plant called the water chestnut that continues to spread throughout Upstate New York's waterways. This plant (not to be confused with the starchy corms of an aquatic sedge used in Chinese cooking) was probably brought to the United States as a water-garden ornamental from its native lands of Asia and Europe.

One of the first places it was seen flourishing in the wild was on the eastern Mohawk River, where today vast, dense mats of the pest cover the shallows. Water chestnut plants are a serious impediment to navigation. In the Hudson River and on the New York canal system, big patches of the tough, stringy surface rosettes often break loose and float over the surface, ready to snare any unwary boater by fouling his or her prop. Water chestnut is also called the "water caltrop," because of its formidable nut-like seed. (Caltrops are those spiny weapons of defense dating back to Roman Empire days, when they were used to disable calvary mounts.) It is now present in more than 60 percent of the state's waterways and continues to spread.

Above: The rosette is a small part of the water chestnut, as underwater growth may extend fifteen or twenty feet down to the bottom. *Photo by Susan P. Gateley.*

Opposite: The water chestnut is also known as water caltrop, thanks to its spiny seed. *Wikipedia.*

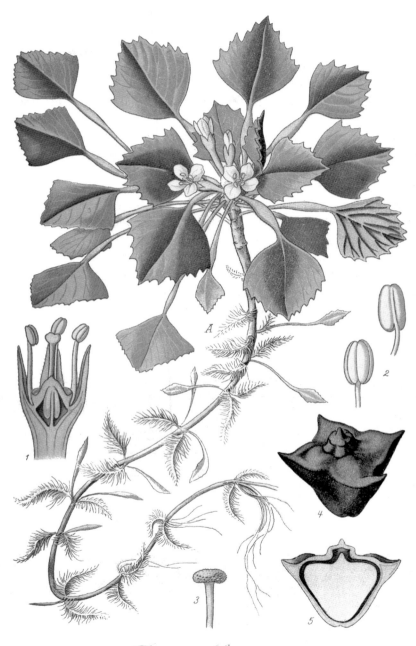

344. Trapa natans L.

Hand-pulling of water chestnut is effective only where the infestation is small. This effort, organized by a local nonprofit group, was photographed in Red Creek Marsh. *Photo by Susan P. Gateley.*

This plant first came to my attention when a few of its distinctive rosettes of leaves appeared on the surface of a marsh near my home. Within two years, those isolated plants had completely covered the water as they choked the creek with their tangled vegetation. The dense foliage of the surface rosette blocks sunlight from reaching the bottom to nourish other plants and the animal life that feeds on them. In extreme cases, the shaded water's oxygen content can drop as photosynthesis decreases. This, to say the least, seriously disrupts the marsh food chain and general web of life, historically a diverse and highly productive one. Water chestnut thrives in nutrient-rich, polluted areas with an excess of nitrogen and phosphorous. Unfortunately, most of our lake's tributaries and wetlands are well fertilized, making them ideal habitat for the weed. Neither native fish nor waterfowl are able to make use of the plants, and it's impossible to paddle a kayak or a canoe through the stuff.

To keep waterways open, paddlers often get together to do water chestnut pulls, manually removing the isolated plants before they spread. On a large scale, the only solutions to removal currently are herbicides and weed cutting, and various state and local entities have spent over $1 million over the last few years clearing the plants from the Oswego River alone.

However, a small leaf beetle native to the same area as the water chestnut, *Gallerucella birmanica*, is now being tested as a biological control of the plant. It has shown promise, but ongoing trials are essential to be sure the beetle won't also target native plants.

The Cormorant

Is the controversial double-crested cormorant an invasive species? It depends on whom you ask. The goose-sized black cormorant, John J. Audubon wrote, has "no song to charm." Rather, the birds fly and float in silence, wary dark beings of stealth, quick to dive if you so much as look at them while passing by in a boat. They sit low in the water; at a distance, you might mistake one for a loon. However, their necks are longer and thinner and they usually hold their bill up at a bit of an angle. Their strong direct flight is businesslike; their skill and grace as powerful underwater swimmers is mostly unseen; and when they vocalize among themselves on a roost, it's in a strange, guttural, grunting, mumbling and croaking language. And almost nobody likes them. Bird-watchers complain that cormorants out-compete other fish-eating birds on rookery islands largely by spreading their acid, tree-killing guano on and around everyone and everything. Anglers complain that they eat far too many valuable fish, and people with moored boats and docks that have been whitewashed by one of the goose-sized fish-eaters complain about the smelly cleanup job.

But you have to give them credit for their comeback on Lake Ontario. Many people think they are native to the lake. Author Farley Mowatt recalled in his book *The Dog Who Wouldn't Be* an expedition to band the birds on Scotch Bonnet Island in the 1930s. However, they were all but extinct by 1970, and I never saw one on fresh water much before the mid-1980s. Today, many people think they are far too abundant.

Cormorants are more sensitive to toxic chemicals than are the lake's ubiquitous ring-billed and herring gulls, and their population on Lake Ontario was down to a few dozen birds in the 1970s, thanks to endocrine-disrupting toxins like PCBs and dioxin and pesticides in the food chain. The few birds that did manage to survive often showed grotesque deformities, including twisted bills, misshapen feet and missing eyes. Because of their high visibility, the mutant birds conveyed a powerful message of the need for government regulation of pesticide use. We owe them a debt of gratitude for that.

The bird on the right has his wings spread to dry his plumage. *Photo by Susan P. Gateley.*

Today, they number in the thousands, dramatic and visible evidence of a cleaner, less-toxic lake. In 1974, about twenty pairs nested on Little Galloo Island. Today, perhaps four thousand pairs use the low-lying island. And they continue to scout out new territory. Last summer, at least two dozen nests appeared in the willows growing on a barrier bar near my home port on Little Sodus Bay. Since it was a high-water year, I wondered if perhaps some birds had been flooded out on their island nesting grounds on Little Galloo.

A few years ago, I spent a couple of nights on a mooring in Toronto's Tommy Thompson Park near what is said to be the largest cormorant colony in North America. More than sixty thousand birds were estimated to occupy this small, artificially enhanced sand spit in 2018. Here they nest on the ground and in the island's cottonwood trees by the thousands, where, despite human harassment, Newcastle disease and fire ants, they produce more cormorants every year. The park's personnel have managed to convince a large percentage of the birds to nest on the ground, helping to reduce damage to trees. But city anglers still complain about the competition for perch and bass. Since each adult bird can catch a pound or more of fish a day (some of which is regurgitated to feed its young), the anglers do have a point.

The rookery in this Toronto city park is one of the largest in North America. *Photo by Susan P. Gateley.*

Various acts of hostility against cormorants, along with occasional outright murder, have been perpetrated by fishermen. The internet tells of an angler on Lake Huron who released a pack of raccoons to eat their eggs on one rookery island. And here on Lake Ontario, on Little Galloo Island back in 1998, sport fishermen killed hundreds of cormorant chicks. Canada has proposed making the fishy-tasting, all-but-inedible cormorant a game bird, allowing up to fifteen a day to be shot during fall hunting season. While cormorants do have adverse impacts on other fish-eating birds on rookery islands, the side effects of willful slaughter of the birds are not pleasant to consider. Almost certainly, cormorants and other innocent birds will suffer from the culling process and its "collateral damage." Some control advocates suggest egg oiling as a less socially disruptive measure than using the birds as living targets, and the New York Department of Environmental Conservation has oiled eggs on Little Galloo in the past. Thinking of the damaged but still-living geese and ducks that appear each fall on my waters during the shotgun season, I would certainly be in favor of more humane control methods than shotguns.

Do they really hurt the fishery? The evidence is mixed and as yet not conclusive. Cormorants eat what's available, mostly in the three- to five-inch range. Often it's alewives. Sometimes it's juvenile drum, walleye, bass, perch or other game fish. In recent years, on Lake Ontario, the round goby, itself a fish with a PR problem, has a favored prey at some locations. One observer remarked that if cormorants were the same snow-white color as the egret, they probably would suffer from much less persecution.

Cormorants aren't as charismatic in flight as are the lake's terns, ospreys or bald eagles. They don't raise their voices in soul-stirring cries like the loon, and they won't snatch a piece of bread tossed at them as a gull in flight can. But if you are lucky enough to stand on a high bank on a quiet fall day and see them swimming underwater in the clear shallows, you have to admire their hunting skills and their extreme maneuverability as they seek out the little fish hidden among the rocks. Pushed by their big webbed feet, their streamlined bodies zip around underwater like small, black torpedoes. With quick efficiency, the birds probe their long, slender bills under and around big rocks, then rocket off to another rock, relentlessly searching out a meal. One with the water, the birds do what their ancestors did long before Lake Ontario even existed. These master fishermen had a place in the aquatic web of life thousands of years before humans created a bone hook or a fishing weir.

FUTURE HISTORY

WHAT ARE WE GOING TO DO WITH ALL THIS FUTURE?

For twenty-five years, I walked on, went swimming from and observed the seasonal changes and small wonders to be found in a section of forested lake shoreline belonging to my in-laws. In November 2018, it lost its beach. The gravel, sand and cobbles disappeared a year after the first record high water of 2017. As I write this in the fall of 2020, the beach is still AWOL, and the erosion and degradation of the property's adjacent marsh and shoreline bluff have accelerated profoundly. At the time of my writing, lake levels were about a foot above longtime averages, but adjacent properties a few miles to the east of us still had their beaches. There is little doubt in my mind that climate change has a lot to do with the disappearance of "my" beach.

A recent article in the *New York Times* stated that a majority of Americans in a given location do not feel that they have experienced personal impacts from global warming. Stronger hurricanes, more frequent hundred-year floods, more record-breaking hot spells or more intense wildfires are happening far away from Lake Ontario's shores. However, the recent record high water on the lake in 2019 was almost certainly directly related to the loss of sea ice and warming of the Arctic. Consensus in the scientific community has been built (and continues to accumulate) for evidence of blocked or stalled weather systems caused by Arctic warming that in turn has been caused by excess greenhouse gases in the atmosphere. Increasingly detailed data fed into computer models shows that as temperature differences between the Arctic and middle latitudes decline, meanders in the polar jet stream develop. The jet normally moves our continent's weather from west to east. When the jet takes a big bend, weather system movement slows or stalls. Persistent patterns of weather result, and days of rain, weeks or months of drought, lengthy hot spells or long periods of winter deep freeze prevail.

In 2017, record rainfall in the upper Midwest from stalled weather filled up the Great Lakes and drenched eastern Ontario Province, and we saw the highest water levels since records began on Lake Ontario. Our lake's water is somewhat regulated by a dam on the St. Lawrence located near Cornwall, Ontario. But flooding from the Ottawa River that enters the St. Lawrence at Montreal limited the dam operators' ability to release water from the lake because of high water downstream. Even so, Canadian cottage residents and basement apartment dwellers in the city suffered from severe flooding. Citizens, first responders and even Ottawa city clerks and secretaries were called out for emergency sand bagging along the Ottawa River. Meanwhile, New York shoreline and bayfront residents with flooded yards and local village and town politicians began blaming President Barack Obama (who was no longer in office), the New York governor, the tree huggers and, most of all, the International Joint Commission's Plan14 for managing water levels on the lake. Very few homeowners blamed God. And they applied in record numbers for permits to harden their shoreline.

As we have already seen in chapter 6, when shoreline erosion stops, so, too, does the transport of beach-building sediment. Although I have

Record high water flooded boatyards and businesses, forcing owners to spend hundreds of thousands of dollars on repairs and remediation. *Photo by Susan P. Gateley.*

found no data on the amount of new shoreline hardening during 2018, I was told that a record number of permits for hardening were issued by DEC, and I can see at least a half-dozen examples of newly placed stone in my immediate neighborhood. It seems inevitable that some reduction of sediment movement has occurred, and I suspect my lost beach is the result. Will it ever return? Perhaps, once a gravel bar is rebuilt by sediment across the mouth of an adjacent creek and wetland. But that protective bar has yet to reappear after almost two years, and it looks like what sediment does move along the shore from the west is being diverted by wave action into the now-open marsh. It could be quite a while before the creek again closes off and stops acting as a sediment sink.

Climate change has been called the Great Intensifier. It is now impacting our lake in a variety of ways, working with other stressors to contribute to a general decline in the lake's well-being and water quality. Since the 1970s, records show reduced ice cover on all the Great Lakes. This in turn has reduced or eliminated the formation of so-called anchor ice along the shore. When the piled-up masses of ice no longer act as a seasonal seawall to protect the shore during winter storms and heavy surf, erosion and siltation of nearshore waters accelerates.

Reduced ice cover on the lake and bays also impacts some of the lake's native fishes. A number of fish species, including the various lake herrings and the whitefish, spawn in areas where protective cover of ice is crucial to the survival of their eggs. One study showed that without frozen water, mortality of fish larvae increased more than threefold. Less ice cover also impacts the seasonal movements of animals like foxes, deer and mice that otherwise could cross frozen bays and rivers to colonize islands and new areas. And less ice means more open water to evaporate during the winter. This in turn feeds into the lake-effect snow machine. More winter snow might make the snowmobilers and the taverns that serve them happy, but it also adds to the cost of keeping the roads clear for taxpayers to get to their jobs, even as greater amounts of road salt runoff causes problems for marshland creatures and contaminates the wells of rural homeowners. Less ice cover could even lead to lower lake levels in the future, since some of the lake-effect snow falls outside our watershed and so is removed from the system.

Global warming is also contributing to more intense weather events, including record rainfalls. So-called hundred-year storms are now occurring every twenty-five years, and when they do, more runoff with farm nutrients and soil loss follows. When those nutrients end up in Lake Ontario or in

The remains of a willow that helped protect the creek were still visible a year after the bar where it grew washed away. *Photo by Susan P. Gateley.*

its bays and creeks, more frequent toxic cyanobacteria blooms and more botulism outbreaks are likely. Pollution of our nation's waterways from too much fertilization is one of the biggest water-quality issues affecting our lakes. Farm field runoff linked to toxic blue-green blooms costs cities millions of dollars in added drinking-water treatment. In Toledo, Ohio, $65 million was spent after toxic algae shut down the city's drinking-water treatment plant in a single event that happened in 2014. That same year, thirty-eight states reported experiencing such blooms annually in their waters.

Flooding, along with a general warming trend, also provides new opportunities for the movement of invasive fish, like various Asian carp species or the northern snakehead, a voracious predator that has gone native in the Potomac. More invasives almost certainly will further simplify and destabilize the web of life in the lake. And six-inch rainfalls will increasingly overwhelm city drainage and sewage systems. Without costly major upgrades to the waste-treatment plants, the problem will get worse.

Another result of flooding will be increased erosion of protective earth and clay caps that now seal dozens of "legacy" waste sites on and near the lake.

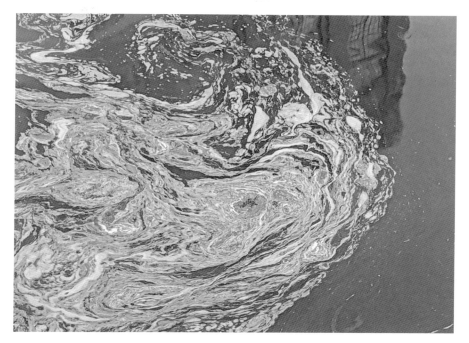

The Oswego River receives agricultural runoff and overflow from City of Syracuse storm drains during heavy rainfalls. *Photo by Susan P. Gateley.*

Some of these sites contain radioactive wastes dating back to the Manhattan Project. Others along the Niagara River, like the infamous Love Canal dump site, contain a witches' brew of chemical toxins. None of this stuff will help the lake's health or that of the people living near it if it enters the water.

Milder winters also allow a greater survival of white-tailed deer within the lake's watershed. Deer browse on seedling trees and brush in the winter and are already impacting the ability of local forests to regenerate. Healthy forests are key to good water quality in Lake Ontario's watershed. With fewer trees and less understory vegetation, the ability of the forest to filter and absorb water from downpours is reduced. More rapid "flashy" runoff, more erosion and more stress on adjacent wetlands and waters is the inevitable result. The sunlit shallows of the lake are major nursery areas for fish. Excessive siltation smothers the life of these shallows.

Some observers are saying that two nearly back-to-back years of record high-water levels in 2017 and 2019 on Lake Ontario appear to confirm model predictions that climate change will generally make our area warmer and wetter. Even as we get wetter, however, other areas in North America appear to be getting drier. It seems inevitable that those areas may seek water from outside sources, including perhaps from the largest freshwater ecosystem in the world. Past suggested schemes to divert water from the Great Lakes for irrigation and export to other nations aboard tanker ships resulted in an agreement among the Great Lakes states to prevent diversions of our water. (Commercial for-profit water-bottling plants are currently exempt.) The agreement is among states, however, and it seems all but certain that it could be overridden by a determined federal government in the event of a severe drought and subsequent food crisis in the Midwest or elsewhere.

The list of interacting factors associated with climate change and stress on Lake Ontario's health is far more extensive than these few examples. Perhaps the most profound impact on our lake's future history, however, will be from the movement of humans responding to climate change. A recent study published by ProPublica states that within fifty years one to three billion people worldwide may be forced to move from their homes as the climate conditions that have served humanity well over the past six thousand years cease to prevail. If current models of changing conditions continue to hold, millions of Americans will almost certainly end up in the moderate climate of the northeastern United States. More than fifty million people live in coastal areas that are already experiencing rising sea levels related to climate change. Floods, constant high tides and storm surges and, in the western United States, wildfires, are now impacting the insurance industry. If home buyers and businesses can't afford insurance or are unable to finance their uninsured purchases, the trillion-dollar-a-year real estate industry will collapse in those areas. That in turn will devastate the rest of the economy. It's likely to also affect those folks lucky enough to still have a house, a pension or a checking account balance.

The same study projected that high temperatures in the Sunbelt, especially when combined with rising humidity levels, would make vast swaths of the South and Southwest uninhabitable. And while climate change projections suggest that higher temperatures in Lake Ontario's watershed may increase corn and soy yields, in other major commodity-crop production areas of the Midwest and Southwest, yields may drop by 50 percent or more.

Already the concept of our area as a climate change "refuge" has appeared on the radar of some who live in our watershed, among them real estate investors. A recent Canadian newspaper echoed the idea with this thought: "Policy makers thinking about sustainable building practices and saving energy, please continue, but add into that how we're going to accommodate the potential flood of climate migrants who will want to move to our regions."

Drought, projected to intensify within the next few decades in the Southwest, is a particularly ugly force that has destroyed many societies. Military intelligence analysts report that drought displaced farmworkers who moved into urban areas of Syria, contributing greatly to the unrest and eventual civil war of that region. Here in the United States, dry spells now cause annual losses nearing $9 billion. It looks increasingly likely that global warming will cause multi-decade "mega-droughts" in parts of the United States within the next thirty to fifty years.

It seems inevitable that within a few decades millions of Americans will be forced to move thanks to climate change. And it looks increasingly likely that some of them will end up in our lake-moderated region, leading to further strains on the lake's ecosystem.

One way humans adapt to drought is by building more municipal systems to extract and distribute groundwater. It should be obvious that protecting groundwater resources from overuse is critical. While historically the Northeast has not experienced widespread shortages of groundwater, that could change. History shows that Americans have long exploited various natural resources aggressively for profit with the repeated mantra of "We'll never run out of 'X'." Substitute whales, cod, white pine trees, great auks or American buffalo for "X," and you get the picture. No doubt, the decision to begin sucking the Aral Sea dry to irrigate cotton fields in central Asia was made by someone who thought the Lake Erie–sized waterbody would supply their needs forever. It only took forty years to turn 90 percent of the lake bottom into dust-swept desert. Unfortunately, we also know that voters and policy makers often fail to recall the lessons of history.

People like David Attenborough, who are way smarter and more knowledgeable about the way the world works than your author, think there is still reason for hope. "What's beautiful about the human species is that we have the free will to decide our own fate," said Ilona Otto, a climate scientist at the Wegener Center for Climate and Global Change. "We have the agency to take courageous decisions and do what's needed," she said. "If we choose."

We can choose.

In the 1970s, after Lake Erie's famous Cuyahoga River caught fire, we chose to limit pollution through the Clean Water Act. And by choosing less-persistent pesticides, we made it possible for the bald eagle, the common loon and the merganser and the osprey to become common on the lake again. We have many tools in the toolbox to reduce the deadly impacts of climate change. One of the most powerful may be changing the way we eat.

Our Great Lakes and our nation stand on the brink of great change. *Author collection*.

Few things would help Lake Ontario's water quality more than reducing the amount of meat and dairy in our diet and choosing to eat organic. Another action that many feel would fight climate change with great rapidity and effect is to implement a meaningful carbon tax.

One other change we could make is to recall the lessons of history. In the time of the indigenous peoples who lived here, water was viewed not as a "right" and a profit-making product but as something to be used and shared by all of the villagers. The clan grandmothers were the water keepers, and it was they who guarded the purity of the resource for children to come. We who live here now should do no less.

We are on the brink of a time of great change. Will we make the right choices?

LAST WORD

PLACES TO EXPLORE THE SHORE

Dozens of public-access points to Lake Ontario beaches, marshlands and forests exist between Rochester and Henderson Harbor. Some, like the Wildlife Management Areas (WMA) under the management of the New York Department of Environmental Conservation, are state owned; some are village or county parks; and some, like El Dorado or Derby Hill, are owned by the Nature Conservancy or other private nonprofits. What follows are a few of my favorites, all of which contain at least some lightly developed shoreline. A number of these locations involve a hike through grass and brush, so be aware of ticks and Lyme disease. I am a great believer in Permethrin sprayed on clothes and hiking shoes. But keep items treated with tick repellent away from your cat!

As described in the book, lake levels drop after midsummer, so fall and winter are great times for exploring the widest beaches of the year. Summer visitors should take note that, except for Fair Haven State Park, these beaches have official "no swimming" policies, as they don't have lifeguards. Use your common sense. Most of the parks have policies about dogs on leashes. Many of the lakeshore marsh units have a way to get to the beach, though routes to the water are not always obvious or easy. The WMA's allow hunting, so check the DEC website for hunting season dates. Use caution, as these are public areas that may attract considerable hunting pressure at times. Most of these sites have online descriptions, and they all have directions to parking areas.

Black Pond Wildlife Management Area

Here you will find a remote and wild sand beach protecting marshlands. To the north lie the limestone ledges of the Nature Conservancy property. I haven't been there since the high water of 2019 and am told that parts of the boardwalk were damaged by wave action. Southwick State Park immediately south of Black Pond is another good access point.

Sterling Nature Center Cayuga County Park

This is an absolute gem with over one thousand acres of forest and old-field habitat, two miles of gravel beach and a bluff to hike on the west side of the park. Great spring wildflowers and very easy access to a shoreline are features, along with ten miles of trails, including a trail around a small buttonwood swamp and another to a big beaver wetland with a heron rookery. One trail wanders along the outlet to the beaver swamp, and you may well see one of the resident rodents out and about here.

Fair Haven Beach State Park

Sitt's Bluff area features good sandy beach access that is very popular on hot summer weekends. The park also has a lightly used trail onto Sitt's Bluff for some spectacular views of the lake and adjacent Sterling Nature Center shoreline.

West Barrier Bark Park Village of Fair Haven

This site is unusual in that you can access both bay and lake. You can drive to the channel jetty maintained by the federal government and walk out to the end of the structure. The east pier featured an osprey nest on the pierhead light for several seasons. The small village park has an interesting mix of native and nonnative vegetation and consists of an artificially enhanced barrier bar that has collected behind the west pier.

Sitt's Bluff, part of Fair Haven Beach State Park. *Photo by Susan P. Gateley.*

RED CREEK MARSH WMA

This can be reached via Larkin and Broadway Road bridges. This is one of the DEC's Lake Shore Marshes management area units. The "lakeshore complex" is composed of seven separate marsh and forest units bounded on the north by Lake Ontario. All together, they consist of approximately 6,179 acres of wetlands and adjacent upland forest and old field. All of the area is available for public use. The DEC website has directions to parking areas that provide access to trails. Look online for New York Lakeshore Marshes WMA for information.

One of the units includes the Scotts Bluff overlook and shore access, located on the east side of the Red Creek Marsh. Here you will find an informal trail down to the one-mile-long pebble beach that protects the marsh from the open lake. The same marsh is spanned by two bridges, one on Broadway, the other on Larkin Road for fishing or boating access. Both bridges have a small gravel launch ramp for small-boat launches. It is best to go paddling here in late fall or before mid-June, when the water weeds can get thick. Scotts Bluff overlook is popular among bird-watchers during the spring raptor migration.

You can reach the west side of Red Creek marsh via Harnden Road, with parking at the old North Wolcott cemetery. Hike a half mile or so north to the lake along an old farm road that is sometimes mowed by DEC. You'll find a ninety-foot bluff for a good overlook of the lake. This is a good place to visit in late fall or early spring, when the leaves are down; there are great views of the north end of the marsh at these times. Bushwhack through the brush down a steep slope to get to the beach. There is plenty of opportunity to pick up a tick during warmer times!

BEAVER CREEK WMA

Located in the town of Wolcott, known as "Dutch Street" to the locals, this site is reached via Dutch Street and includes an upland forest where Girl Scouts Camp Whistlewood introduced your author and others to the delights of overnight camping. The creek and marsh are protected by a barrier bar from the lake and are a paddler's delight in spring or fall.

Chimney Bluffs State Park, a couple miles east of Sodus Bay, is a popular access area to the lake. *Photo by Susan P. Gateley.*

Chimney Bluffs State Park

This is a largely undeveloped state park located a couple miles east of Sodus Bay and features the highest clay cliffs on the south shore. Trails run through the hardwoods, and during normal lake levels, there is usually good beach access here off of East Bay Road that runs along East Bay (another good area to explore with a car topper boat).

Camp Beechwood State Park and Maxwell Creek

The former Girl Scouts camp here features a wide variety of habitats for birders to exploit and a magnificent small stand of old-growth beach, oak, maple and tulip poplar trees. Maxwell Creek is very popular with fishermen during the spring salmon and trout runs and has a parking area for angler use on the east side.

Additional noteworthy sites for nearshore exploration east of Rochester include the Derby Hill Bird Observatory (no beach access) and the Webster Park and Whiting Road / Gosnell's Big Woods Preserve town parks in Webster. Check www.webstertrails.org for information on these facilities.

BIBLIOGRAPHY

Charlevoix, Pierre. *A Voyage to North America*. Wikipedia. https://en.wikipedia.org.

Clinton, DeWitt. *Life and Writings His Private Canal Journal*. www.eriecanal.org.

Egan, Dan. *The Death and Life of the Great Lakes*. New York: W.W. Norton, 2017.

Eyles, N., A. Zajc, A. and M. Doughty. "High-Resolution Seismic Sub-Bottom Reflection Record of Low Hypsithermal Levels in Ontario Lakes." *Journal of Great Lakes Research* 41 (2015): 41–52.

Fossils of Upstate New York. www.thefossilforum.com.

Gateley Susan P. *The Edgewalker's Guide to Lake Ontario Beach Combing*. Wolcott, NY: Whiskey Hill Press, 2003.

———. *Maritime Tales of Lake Ontario*. Charleston, SC: The History Press, 2012.

———. *Saving the Beautiful Lake*. Wolcott, NY: Whiskey Hill Press, 2015.

Great Lakes Sea Grant. https://greatlakesseagrant.com.

Hatcher, Harlan. *The Great Lakes*. New York: Oxford University Press, 1944.

International Centre for Waterspout Research. Facebook page.

Jesuit Relations, 1632–1673. Annual Chronicles of the Jesuit Missions in New France. Kripke Center, Creighton University. http://moses.creighton.edu.

Journey North. "Monarch Migration Monitoring." www.journeynorth.org.

Kaufman, Wallace, and Pilkey Orrin. *The Beaches Are Moving*. Norwell, MA: Anchor Press, 1979.

Nelson Daniel A. "Ghost Ships of the War of 1812." *National Geographic* (March 1893): 289–313.

Outwater, Alice. *Water: A Natural History*. New York: Basic Books, 1996.

Pound, Arthur. *Lake Ontario*. Port Washington, NY: Kennikat Press, 1945.

ProPublica. "The Great Climate Migration." www.propublica.org, 2020.

Scott, W.B., and E.J. Crossman. *Freshwater Fishes of Canada Bulletin*, no. 184 (1973).

Spider Identification Community. "Spiders of New York." www.spiderid.com.

Tommy Thompson Park. "Cormorants in Tommy Thompson Park." Toronto and Region Conservation Authority. https://www.tommythompsonpark.ca.

Toronto and Region Conservation Authority. "Cormorants in Tommy Thompson Park." www.trca.ca.

Van Diver, Bradford B. *Roadside Geology of New York*. Missoula, MT: Mountain Press, 1985.

Wegener Center for Climate and Global Change. https://wegcenter.uni-graz.at/en/wegener-center.

ABOUT THE AUTHOR

Susan P. Gateley, a native Upstate New Yorker, has authored a half dozen books on Lake Ontario, including two for Arcadia Publishing, since 1979. She has an MS in fisheries and has been a sailor and lake watcher for half a century. In 2015, she and her husband released a one-hour documentary on Lake Ontario through Ariel Associates, *Quest for Hope*. The video is based on her nonfiction book *Saving the Beautiful Lake*. Find it and links to two other short videos at her website, where her books that are currently in print are also listed. Here, too, is a link to her blog on Lake Ontario with notes and photos on line since 1995.

www.susanpgateley.com

Visit us at
www.historypress.com